I0413067

REALITIES

OF

SELF-EDITING

MISTI WOLANSKI

First Edition
Copyright 2015
All Rights Reserved

The information presented in this book stems from the author's own experiences and opinions, and your use of this book means you accept that she's as fallible as anyone else. Any and all websites, authors, and books references do not necessarily indicate any affiliation or agreement, express or implied, between the author and the reference, unless the author is referencing one of her own works. In which case, the connection between the two is obvious. Any and all affiliate links herein only mean that I find that source or vendor particularly worth using, not that I recommend that item or vendor because of its affiliate program.

Translation: *There's no such thing as a perfect book, and this is no exception. I also refer to other people and their products, and when I particularly like a product or a vendor, I sign up for its affiliate program. That doesn't mean those other people agree with or even like me. So don't assume they share my opinions, that I necessarily share theirs, or that this book is perfection embodied. Thank for understanding. ^_^*

Cover designed by Misti Wolanski
Photo © adam121 at Kozzi.com
Alegreya font © Juan Pablo del Peral of Huerta Tipográfia
Amatic font © Vernon Adams of NewTypography.co.uk

TABLE OF CONTENTS

A FEW GRAMMAR NOTES

I have a few grammar preferences that are considered wrong in some circles. Please be aware that if you follow my lead on any of these, you may wrongfully get accused of incompetence, despite these decisions being entirely logical and completely defensible.

What grammar preferences are those, you ask?

I intentionally use "they" and "their" instead of the clunky "he or she" and "his or her" in cases of unknown gender. There are linguistic and historic reasons for doing this. (Namely, "their" has long been plural and singular, which can be proven by looking to classic literature.)

I follow UK grammar rules for where I place my commas and periods with quotation marks. (Per US grammar, periods and commas are almost always supposed to go within quotation marks, even when not part of the original quote. UK grammar says to only do that if the periods and commas are part of the original quote.) I also use the UK rules for abbreviations (no periods), and the presumably UK "towards", etc.; although I'm 100% USian, that's what I and my friends say.

For other things, I pretty much follow Chicago Manual of Style, 16th edition, though I format suspension points (usually called "ellipses") like em dashes.

If you encounter something that's consistently "wrong", I ask you to bear in mind that some details of correct spelling and grammar differ depending on your dictionary, handbook, and region. Thanks to the Internet, the reading world has gone global. I see no reason to stick to downright confusing rules unique to US grammar.

Other than that, I apologize for any typos or issues that have slipped through the editing.

FOREWORD

I could describe all my credentials that make me qualified to speak on editing, but that's simply irrelevant. You're reading this book either because you believe me when I say I know what I'm talking about, or because you think I'm full of it.

You're entitled to your opinion, and nothing I claim is likely to dissuade you of that opinion, even though particular titles I've edited have ended up on bestseller lists. After all, how much an editor influences a person's place on sales charts is debatable.

So let's move on…

With self-publishing's return to viability, and with freelancing also getting more widely accepted, I find myself at an impasse.

As a self-employed writer, I'm expected to adequately edit my own work, so anything I submit is ready for publication.

For as a self-employed editor, I'm expected to say that it's impossible for writers to adequately edit their own work.

That contradiction bothers me.

So, with that in mind, I ran a mini-series on my blog about self-editing, answering such questions as:

- Is it possible to adequately edit your own work?

- Is it advisable to adequately edit your own work?

- Is it professional to edit your own work?

- What does an editor do, anyway?
  (And what should they be doing?)

You see, I'm a self-publishing author. (Obviously.)
But...

I'm also a freelancer—a freelance writer **and** line editor. (So, no, not all line editors lack the skillz to write their own books. It just so happens that the things that make me good at ghostwriting also make me good at line editing, and I enjoy both things. I also have an active aversion to letting only one skill pay all my bills—and I easily become bored when I'm doing the same type of work all the time.)

I also do some basic web coding—and that's an interesting field in itself, because "self-editing" (called "debugging" or "parsing" in the world of coding) is standard. It's often even easiest to debug code you yourself wrote, because everyone has their own...quirks in how they format and arrange their code.

WHO THIS BOOK IS FOR:

- Anyone who *has* to write, whether you like it or not, who wants to broaden their understanding of what, exactly goes into a professional edit.

This book contains details that apply to everyone from the person who writes company memos to the person in the middle of writing their nineteenth novel. (While I hope the latter person already knows these things, I likely cover some details that even a professional writer won't know, unless they've been a professional editor, too. If you *have* been a professional writer and editor, you'll likely find another resource more worth your time and money.)

WHAT THIS BOOK IS:

- An overview of what's involved in editing a book, for writers who need or want to edit their own work, either for release to their audience (such as co-workers, a teacher, or a publisher) or to minimize the issues in what they submit to their support group (such as an editor, a publisher, or an agent).

Note that a good hired editor can produce a better end product if the editor's good at editing their own work—because then the editor can focus on what would improve the writer's goal for the story, rather than having to focus on merely making the story readable.

- A compilation and expansion of my blog posts on all the various types of editing, what they involve, and methods a writer can use to help themselves edit their own work, adjusted into book form.

In the interest of being true to the original articles, that blog origin will show at times, and I include the discussion question(s) at the end of each article, with the URL given in a footnote so you can join in the conversation. Please feel free to do so. I don't make you jump through hoops to comment, and my comments manager means I'll see your comment, even if it's years after the original blog post.

WHAT THIS BOOK IS NOT:

- A checklist for specific items to do, to edit your own writing.

- A book deriding self-editing as impossible.

- A book lauding self-editing as easy and doable by everyone.

So if you're seeking a checklist for what specifically to edit or how, *this is **not** the book you're looking for.* I don't know what type of editing you need, nor do I know what stage of editing you're on.

A "checklist" book for ***all*** the various types of editing—for all types of writers—would be unwieldy, even self-contradictory, because every writer is different. If you want resources more along those lines, though, I recommend you check out Janice Hardy's blog[1], Jami Gold's blog[2], and Holly Lisle's books[3]. (Full disclaimer: That last link is an affiliate link. I've yet to find a single resource from Holly Lisle that is not worth at least the cover price.)

If you're looking for advice on specific issues you know you're having problems with, *this book is **not** what you're looking for.*

If you're wanting reinforcement of your opinion that failing to have your work edited by a third party is necessarily unprofessional and rude to your audience, *this book is **not** what you're looking for.* (But I address the professionalism of self-

---

[1]   http://fiction-university.com
[2]   http://jamigold.com/
[3]   http://www.howtothinksideways.com/affiliate/idevaffiliate.php?id=3731

editing in the first chapter, so perhaps you might be interested in checking that out.)

If you're wanting someone to pat you on the back and say how great and innovative you are for self-editing and that *of course* everyone can self-edit, *this book is **not** what you're looking for*. You aren't nearly as innovative as you think you are. You're incorrect about that "of course", too.

But if you're wanting an overview of how to approach editing, to help you improve of a writer? This book is for you.

The original blog post series can still be read for free at http://carradee.blogspot.com[4], but this book features revised and expanded editions of those posts.

- For the full list of top resources that I recommend (and some popular ones that I recommend you avoid), please see Appendix A.

- For a list of the various authors and books I reference in this book, please see Appendix B.

Between this book and its appendixes, I hope all readers can readily find what they find most useful in this book.

---

[4] http://carradee.blogspot.com/search/label/Realities of Self-Editing series

PROFESSIONALISM AND THE WRITER

IS SELF-EDITING UNPROFESSIONAL?

Before I answer the question, let's address the feasibility of self-editing. The professionalism of an action means little if the action is itself impossible.

There are two main schools of thought in self-editing:

- Nobody can adequately edit themselves.

- Everybody can (learn to) adequately edit themselves.

My "day job" is as a freelancer. I proofread, write, edit, and write—for small businesses, with small businesses, for individual entrepreneurs, for self-publishers, *as* a self-publisher, etc....

My first freelance job ever, as an eighteen-year-old college chick, was writing online articles, and I was **expected**—required—to *adequately edit my own work*. But now, working as a freelance editor for self-publishing authors, I'm **expected** to insist that *everyone needs an editor*.

I can't be the only one who sees the inconsistency there.

Business writers, students writing term papers and test essays, professionals writing their own e-mails—all of them must edit and proofread their own work. Okay, in some cases, editing can be outsourced to a lackey, but on a test essay? My best essay grade in college was one where I was given the topic and had an hour to produce that essay. My teacher gave me a 99% and later apologized for not giving me 100%, because she hadn't found any errors and the essay still resounded with her.

(You may be thinking, "But wait! Freelancers go through editors, too!" In my experience, the editors are usually *acquisitions* editors. Acquisitions editors' job is to make sure you nail the tone and angle that the publication wants, not to repair misuse of the English language. Such fixing of your mistakes is the realm of line editors, copyeditors, and proofreaders—and what each type fixes actually differs, depending on a lot of factors that I'll address later.)

As far as college students' need for editors, one university I attended doesn't allow any of its students to get editing help beyond "You have comma splices in your paper." If someone does mark the actual errors in a student's paper, that student can get expelled for cheating.

Yup. *Expelled*. With an editor marking up your paper counting as *cheating*.

That university has a few thousand attendees every year, and every one of them is required to attend—and pass—at least one writing course in order to continue their schooling. Every class uses the selfsame textbooks, worksheets, assignments, grading system—all of it. (Students are also required to pass a speech class, but... Yeah, that's as much a pain as it sounds. I hated that class.)

So that's one entire university, where the entire system is built with the premise that students *can* adequately edit their own work.

Self-publishers, though, are often told that they're being "unprofessional" if they don't hire editors and proofreaders for their manuscript.

Cognitive dissonance[5], much?

While I agree that the majority of writers need **or** can benefit from hiring good editors—and a proofreader is usually a good idea—I disagree that hiring an editor makes someone "professional".

Hiring an editor doesn't do you diddle-squat if you don't understand what that editor's supposed to be doing—nor if your editor doesn't actually do their job.

A (near-)"flawless" manuscript isn't what makes you a "professional," either.

Look at Amanda Hocking[6]. She's a nice girl, polite and treating her writing like the business it is. But all the editors she hired—and she hired *more than one*—evidently didn't catch something in her *My Blood Approves* series that struck me as a large plot hole, which could've been fixed with a few tweaks. (I still read all four and don't mind recommending them to people who enjoy that kind of paranormal romance, but I wouldn't dare recommend them to a reader convinced all teen paranormal romance is crap, because that reader would likely consider her a case in point, missing the reason Ms. Hocking became so popular as a self-published author: she's a fantastic storyteller.)

Am I to consider her "unprofessional" because her works aren't "flawless"?

Look at Dean Wesley Smith[7] and Kristine Kathryn Rusch[8], longtime writers (who are married to each other), who probably have more stories under each penname than I have

---

5   http://en.wikipedia.org/wiki/Cognitive_dissonance
6   http://www.worldofamandahocking.com/
7   http://www.deanwesleysmith.com/
8   http://kriswrites.com/

ideas. They know what they want to do with their writing, and they're more concerned about getting quality stories out there in *enjoyable* form than in *flawless* form. They do what they can to put stuff out as error-free as possible, but they don't stress over trying to make the story perfect. (See Smith's[9] and Rusch's[10] own words about that.) As of this writing, Rusch is the only person to win a Hugo award for both her writing and editing, and both of them have been writers, editors, *and* publishers.

Am I to consider these two "unprofessional" because they don't even aim for technically "flawless" stories?

Or am I to consider "perfect" writing a myth?

Merriam-Webster is **the** dictionary of choice in US publishing. (Some specific fields use other dictionaries, but overall, Merriam-Webster is the default for the US; Oxford is the default for elsewhere.) The pertinent definition of *professional* (2a) is "participating for gain or livelihood in an activity or field of endeavor often engaged in by amateurs" (according to the unabridged online dictionary[11]).

Professionalism is "the conduct, aims, or qualities that characterize or mark a profession or a professional person" (same source, definition 1a). So what makes you professional is how you behave and what you want out of your chosen profession.

Therefore, "professionalism" a matter of *attitude*, an attitude of seeking financial return from your chosen profession. (You don't have to be "professional" and seek

---

[9]   http://www.deanwesleysmith.com/?p=1826
[10]   http://kriswrites.com/2012/06/27/the-business-rusch-perfection/
[11]   http://unabridged.merriam-webster.com/

financial return from your writing if you don't want to—but I'll get more into that in the next chapter.)

A professional freelance writer, one who wants to make money by writing, **must** self-edit and self-proofread to get assignments, unless they seek clueless clients. (Which does happen, and I feel sorry for the misled clients.)

A professional author, on the other hand, can edit themselves, hire editors, or do both. It depends on what they need (and how much they're willing to pay editors). I find many more typos in work by a favorite author of mine who's a *New York Times* bestseller and gets edited by one of the so-called "big" publishers, than I find in my favorite self-publishing authors, some of whom I know don't hire help. (They might use volunteer help, but for competent folks to volunteer to help you, you have to be pretty close to flawless to begin with.)

Now, notice that I'm **not** saying "You must self-edit your story" or "You must hire a pro editor."

I'm saying your choice on whether to self-edit or to hire out editing does not have any bearing on being a *professional*.

What are your thoughts on (self-)editing and professionalism?[12]

---

[12] http://carradee.blogspot.com/2011/11/is-self-editing-unprofessional.html

c.

Must Writers Be Professional?

So, since self-editing is not unprofessional, that leads to the question: *Must* writers be professional?

Let's first recap those pertinent definitions from Merriam-Webster (according to the unabridged online dictionary[13]):

PROFESSIONAL

participating for gain or livelihood in an activity or field of endeavor often engaged in by amateurs (definition 2a)

PROFESSIONALISM

the conduct, aims, or qualities that characterize or mark a profession or a professional person (definition 1a)

Ergo, if you're seeking financial return from your writing, you're a professional writer*. If you don't care about the financial return, you're not a professional writer.

Notice that there's no time limitation in that definition. Someone who has a plan for financial return in the long run *despite a plan for **no** financial return in the short term* would still count as a professional.

But **must** writers be professionals?

---

[13] http://unabridged.merriam-webster.com/

In self-publishing, in freelancing, there's a common attitude that you **must** be professional, else you shouldn't be writing.

Funny. It was my dabbling (for fun) as a teenager that gave me the skills to be what I am now: author, proofreader, tutor, etc. I didn't even know freelancing existed at the time, but I *unprofessionally* wrote articles to help friends, critiqued their papers (and they mine), and proofread everything I saw or heard. (There's a reason my mother started adding "Do NOT proofread this!" to notes she left for me.)

I would spend *hours* teaching basic grammar to fellow fan fiction writers. Some of you readers even know me from way back when (Misti_Whitesun).

I remember reading comments on someone's story, to see someone respond to my own comment: "Oh, don't mind her; she's rude and a little mean." I remember spending a good hour per (short) chapter, critiquing someone's story line-by-line because the author requested it, and the author had to defend me publicly because her other readers came after me.

I was a hobbyist then, even while I was racking up experience that would serve me very well once I switched from a hobbyist to a professional. But should I have not read, edited, or tutored, because I didn't even seek remuneration?

Any hobby has its dabblers. The artist who takes a year to make a painting for a friend. The sculptor who produces clay objects now and again, as desired. The knitter who makes the occasional toy for friends' children. The poet who mainly writes poetry if she forgets to buy a card for a friend's wedding. (Only those last two are me.)

Okay, so friends might tell such creative folks that they should sell their work, but if those creative folks don't want to sell their work, nobody will flip out and ask them why they even bother with their hobby. Nobody will suggest that the hobbyist is undervaluing paintings or pottery or handknit toys.

Whereas a writer who insists on being "unprofessional" and giving their work away for free gets insulted and pressured to *stop writing*.

Why?

Okay, so I suspect I know why. Writers are generally under-appreciated and underpaid. Look at how often writers are pressured to accept "exposure" as appropriate payment for something. (If I want exposure instead of payment, I'll make that call and *volunteer* for it, thanks.) Newbie freelance writers, seeking work online, are often pressured to take paltry amounts of a few cents per word—

And I bet *that* paltry amount, offered to freelance writers, stems from fiction markets. (I know it confused me, when I got started.)

See, for *fiction*, magazines and e-zines are deemed as "pro" 'zines if they pay a minimum of 5¢ per word. A would-be freelancer (or someone looking to hire freelancers) might see that, not realize the distinctions between fiction and nonfiction—or between FNASR and "all rights"—and therefore offer something that seems reasonable to *them*… with it actually being a fraction of standard freelance rates.

Many types of freelancers give up *all* rights to what they produce. Whereas in the fiction world, pro-paying magazines and e-zines usually just take specific rights, with limitations, leaving the author free to resell it further.

Add a "0" to the end of what's generally offered per word for fiction, and you'll be closer to hitting a standard freelance rate for sale of "all rights".

(Speaking of which: Fiction writers, be leery of giving up "all rights" or signing contracts that last for the duration of a story's copyright. It can be appropriate in some situations—as in work-for-hire ghostwriting or writing media tie-in novels—but less so for a story, world, and characters that *you* came up with. Note that I'm not a lawyer, so if you want legal advice, hire the appropriate attorney. I'm just sharing a rule of thumb that's good to keep in mind whether you're a hobbyist or a professional.)

That difficulty many writers have finding respect and appropriate payment for their work probably makes us a wee sensitive when someone waltzes in and says, "I don't care about the money! I just want to be read!"

You know, there are music artists who offer their music free, too, as downloads or just for streaming online. Maybe it's just where I hang out online, but I've only recently heard anyone accusing such artists of devaluing music. (Well, the critiques of Amanda Palmer have been around for longer—but there's more involved in that particular accusation.)

Not everyone's trying to write for their "day job", just like not everyone's trying to paint or sculpt or knit or sing *as a job*. They might do it for fun and share it *for fun*.

So no, I **don't** think writers *must* be professional, whether they write fiction or nonfiction.

But there's another side to this. A dark side. The "information should be free" side, that claims people *shouldn't* demand money for their writing, for their music, for their work.

To those who insist everything is or should be free, I call foul. You pay to eat, don't you? So do I. (And between my allergies and hyperactive thyroid, my food bill is probably as high or higher than yours, even though I mostly cook from scratch. That's not even touching the bills for what I need to keep my health issues in line.)

Therefore while I think writers need not be professional and receive wages from their writing if they don't want to, I also think they have the right to be professional if they want to be.

What's your take on the necessity of professionalism in writers?[14]

* Folks argue over the significance of the terms *writer* and *author*. As far as I'm concerned, a "writer" is someone who writes. An "author" is someone who's been paid by an unbiased third party for their writing, regardless of whether or not they keep writing. Plenty of very smart, professional people define these terms differently, so before entering a discussion about the words (or before taking offense) be sure to check that your definitions don't differ from the other person.

[14] http://carradee.blogspot.com/2011/11/must-writers-be-professional.html

EDITING ABILITY

Editing Ability, Muphry's Law, and the Overconfidence Effect

Now it's time to address a person's *capability* to edit their own work. I've already pointed out the two main schools of thought on that. Some folks (mainly, those involved in *fiction*) believe it's impossible; whereas some (mainly, those involved in *nonfiction*) believe it's possible.

Personally, I believe everyone can *improve* their self-editing skills. I've never yet tutored someone who was unable to learn how to apply grammar better.

But not everyone can self-edit adequately enough to be able to work without an editor. Self-editing requires a very different skill set from storytelling and writing, which not all want or bother to learn. Also, perception handicaps, learning disabilities, and attitude problems can all interfere with how *effective* someone can be.

What do I mean by that?

Let's start with the simplest item that affects your ability to self-edit: **perception handicaps**.

If you're blind, you aren't going to be able to check your formatting. If you're color-blind, your ability to design your own covers is limited, because you might use clashing fire engine red where you meant a nice gray. (About that: The bright pink on my website and on the cover of this book? It's on purpose. I've tested it through "Here's how it looks to the color blind" filters, and it's a color that universally looks nice, even when converted to another color by a person's color blindness.)

I'm *not* calling it bad or wrong to have such handicaps. I *am* saying that if you have a perception handicap, you're going to have limitations in what you can do.

I don't have depth perception, myself. I see no difference between a photo and reality. If I'm off the ground, I can't tell if it's by two feet or twenty. That was one of the reasons I decided to stop climbing trees as a kid, although I enjoyed it: I realized that getting *down* was actually more dangerous for me than it is for most people. (The other reason involved something that made climbing *up* similarly dangerous, but explaining that would be off-topic. Suffice to say that it's only by God's grace that I never killed myself.)

Don't try to force yourself to do something you that you are legitimately incapable of. Everyone has limits. Some of us just have more obvious limits than others.

However, also be careful about what you consider a limitation. Most people are convinced they can't do things that they actually can, if they're taught properly.

The second thing that can interfere with someone's ability to self-edit is **learning disabilities**.

If you're badly dyslexic or have some other verbal processing disorder, then you'll have to work *with* that. (Not 'against'.) How you approach editing, how much work you have to put into it, and how long it takes you can all be affected.

Most teaching styles work *against* those things, making them improper methods for someone with dyslexia or another verbal processing disorder. That assumption that folks with dyslexia necessarily struggle with school is because schools work against dyslexia, which results in incredibly late diagnoses for some students, because they self-correct until others convince them they can't possibly be dyslexic.

I have a very hard time with numbers, myself. If I'm not concentrating, I *will* transpose numbers. (Not 'might'.) And even when I concentrate on what I'm doing, I still transpose numbers a little more frequently than most people—often enough that people notice and comment.

You might therefore think that I never do math in my head. You might therefore think that I struggle with the invoicing and bookkeeping required as a freelancer.

You'd be wrong on both counts. I'm actually very good with math. I understand it rather well.

But my dyscalculia (dyslexia with numbers) affects *how* I do math. I've figured out how to work *with* the condition, rather than trying to force myself to do things "properly".

I always solve a math problem at least twice. If the answers conflict, I try again. Most of the time, the answer I get two out of three times is the right one. (I also often do a rough estimation of what the answer should be, so I can make sure I hit the right ballpark. That's particularly handy when I'm doing division or working with fractions—processes in which transposition dramatically changes the answer.)

Even after I do all that, I also like double-checking my work on a calculator or in a spreadsheet. My spreadsheets have extra "check" columns, that run estimates and flag when things are out of the ordinary.

That's me, knowing a problem I have and working with it to minimize the effects. My mother taught me to read and do basic algebra before I started school, and she's (obviously) an undiagnosed dyslexic, so I was using coping mechanisms from the start.

I was in *college* before anyone noticed my math disability.

I may even be outright dyslexic, judging from what happens to my writing when I'm tired, stressed, or rushed. And yet I'm a successful writer and editor.

But when I was in school, nobody ever bothered to test me, because I was a good student. My learning style is particularly well suited to the standard US schoolroom, and I'd developed coping mechanisms for the issues that remained. My calculus professor noticed and commented, asking because he had no idea how else to explain what I was doing on paper. I could explain everything verbally, but my numbers were jumping all over the place.

If you have learning disabilities that interfere with your ability to self-edit, you'll need to develop your own coping mechanisms. A disability does **not** *necessarily* produce an inability to self-edit.

The third item that can interfere with your ability to self-edit is **attitude**.

I admit that I hadn't heard of Muphry's [sic] Law before I went searching on Wikipedia for the name of the concept I'm going to focus on, but this one also works.

MUPHRY'S LAW

"if you write anything criticizing editing or proofreading, there will be a fault of some kind in what you have written" (Source: Wikipedia[15])

Nobody's perfect. For everything, there's a point where you have to say "It's good enough" and let it go. (See Kris Rusch's post on perfection[16].)

But is that let-go thing actually good enough for general consumption?

I noticed something, even as a teenager when I was hanging out on fan fiction sites (...*and* learning how to give critique, because I'd been taught that positive comments were cruel and rude, but that's kinda off-topic).

As a general rule, the more confident someone was about their writing, the more their writing sucked.

The less confident someone was about their writing, the better it tended to be—until it plateaued at a point where a writer was fairly confident that they could put a sentence together without being convinced that "My writing is *the bestest thing evah*!"

Those coolheaded ones *were* the fantastic storytellers, mind you, but they didn't realize that or even believe it of themselves.

The tendency to overstate your ability in a subject has actually been researched. It's called the "overconfidence effect."

---

[15] http://en.wikipedia.org/wiki/Muphry%27s_law
[16] http://kriswrites.com/2012/06/27/the-business-rusch-perfection/

OVERCONFIDENCE EFFECT

The less you know about a subject, the less you assume there is to know, and the more you overestimate your knowledge of that subject (Source: Wikipedia[17])

So let's try a quick quiz to test if you might be able to self-edit your own work. Answer honestly, now.

1. You know everything there is to know, everything you need to know, and everything you should know about editing.

2. You know a little, but you know that there are many things still need to learn.

3. You know some, but you're not sure you know everything you should.

4. You know a fair bit, though you're sure you don't know everything.

5. You know a lot. You're sure it isn't everything, but you know where to look things up.

Now let's rate your score:

• If you answered 1: Forget it for now. You have a long way to go before being able to edit your own work—an event that can't start until you have an attitude change. Nobody—not even an editor with three decades under their belt—knows *everything*.

---

[17] http://en.wikipedia.org/wiki/Overconfidence_effect

- If you answered 2: Keep heart. You have a way to go, but you're on the right track!

- If you answered 3: Keep at it. You're getting there… (And you might actually be adequate.)

- If you answered 4: Try it out. You might be ready; at any rate, practice will do you good.

- If you answered 5: Get to it. You're a good candidate for self-editing; at worst, you'll clean up your strong points to make it easier for someone else to identify your weak points.

I'm not going to gracefully bow out of this one. I'm an editor for my "day job", so of course I consider myself a 5. But in my own writing, my weakest points are transitions and plotting. (I've also recently noticed that a tendency to end sentences with "though".)

My often transition-less way of thinking even loses folks who know me well, so I have to focus to make sure I connect the dots. (Sometimes I lose *myself*, which can be kinda frightening, to be honest.)

I can also produce individual characters, situations, and scenes that make a pre-reader plea for more, but stringing them together into a *plot*? That's harder for me. (That's part of why I have so many WiPs—some are only characters and situations, right now; no plots.)

Even in day-to-day life, I have a tendency to think too hard. That's part of why I like writing short stories; they make me focus on Ockham's Razor, to produce plots that fit in about a paucity of words.

Regardless of how you answered the quiz, might you be an exception to the above rules of thumb? Possibly. But I can't think of one exception that I've ever encountered in my years of working professionally—if you count my time as a hobbyist, we're well into two-digit territory—so forgive me for being dubious.

You can grow from one position to another, but the key is finding a resource or somebody that connects with you, to help you learn. If you're at level 1–3, I suggest you start poking around Janice Hardy's blog[18].

I recommend avoiding the grammar handbooks until you're at level 4. Many a person has confused themselves because they started reading the grammar handbooks before they had the background to understand them. (Grammar handbooks have a knack for omitting transitions and for specifying things in the examples rather than in the explanatory text.)

Now that you have some idea of if you're a good candidate for self-editing or not, we'll continue, addressing issues like the different types of editing and tricks to help take advantage of your strengths.

How'd you score on the quiz? What are your thoughts on Muphry's Law and the Overconfidence Effect?[19]

---

[18] http://fiction-university.com
[19] http://carradee.blogspot.com/2011/11/editing-ability-muphrys-law-and.html

Two Types of Editors in This World

If you've ever started poking into online information about editing, you've likely discovered that the job descriptions for "editor" are myriad, and they differ from situation to situation. Some editors make sure all the content lines up and the plot works; some ensure that all the commas are in the right places. Some verify your data, while others make sure you're suitable for publication.

But when you get right down to it, there are only two (2) types of editors:

1. "Big picture" editors focus more on the forest than on the trees. This is sometimes called "macroediting".

2. "Little picture" editors focus more on the trees than on the forest. This is sometimes called "microediting".

Content editors are the first type, "big picture" editors. This is also the type of feedback you usually want from your first beta reader. Do I have enough information? Does my argument make sense? Does this story even work? Are my characters believable?

Line editors, copyeditors, and proofreaders are the second type, "little picture" editors. The technical aspects are their forte. Are my mechanics right? Are my transitions in place? Do my characters each stay true to their voices?

A **good** editor of any type will have crossover in what they see, like a copyeditor who notices that your villain speaks like the heroine in one scene—that's a detail catch, but it's based on the big-picture analysis of who your characters are. In nonfiction, your proofreader might notice that your essay's missing a piece of information that would help bring it all together—that's a content editor's job to mention, but a proofreader might still notice. The content editor who says you should study dialogue tags or block quote formatting is noticing a little-picture issue.

But every type of editing is skewed towards the forest or the trees. The skew might be slight, but it'll be there.

For example, take acquisitions editors. Acquisitions editors often don't edit at all, but they make executive determinations about if a piece of writing is worth acquiring or not. They will also lean either way, either as "big picture" or "little picture" people. Both sides of editing will usually be important to them, because they're trying to find a piece to accept. They ideally want to find something that'll fit their publication or company as-is.

But what if an acquisitions editor needs a piece, nothing in the slush pile is ideal, and the choice is down to two pieces? One that's a little weak on the plot (forest) but that they couldn't put down for the beautiful prose (trees), and another that's missing a comma or two (trees) but that they couldn't put down for the compelling story (forest)?

Or maybe it's a nonfiction magazine, and one piece has great mechanics, but it's not quite as cutting-edge as another one that'll need a bit of cleanup.

This subjectivity of value applies to professors, too, if you're writing an essay for a class. That's why it's ideal to get professor feedback on your first essay prior to turning it in, because it'll let you evaluate what the professor's stickler points are, and what points they let slide.

For all those example situations, the better choice depends on the situation, the publication, and the editor's taste. Some acquisitions editors or professors will prefer one; some, the other. That's to be expected.

And there's no such thing as a perfect piece of writing, so every piece of writing could be improved somewhere. That imperfect "somewhere" will be a deal breaker for some editors, but a non-issue for others.

There are also points in which a "flaw" is a matter of taste. My novel *A Fistful of Fire*[20] has fairly odd pacing and a reactive narrator. I know that. But changing it into something else—overhauling the story into something more normal or even just smoothening the flow—would've changed the novel from what I'd meant it to be. Some readers love the story as-is, loving how the pacing fits (though it's not the easiest to delve into). Some readers love the story but tell me they wish the pacing differed or some such thing. Some can't stand it whatsoever and think it sucks.

All those readers are right. The novel isn't perfect—no story is perfect—but it is what it is, and what some readers

---

[20] http://www.amazon.com/gp/product/B004UMG1PC/

love, others hate. What bothers some readers doesn't bother others. That's all normal and to be expected.

I also released that novel knowing full well that it would get those reactions.

Writers I work with know I'm big on having cause before effect in your writing, but I read plenty of books wherein the editor obviously wasn't as bothered by that issue as I am, even though putting the effect before its cause often produces a PoV problem. (Janice Hardy has a blog post[21] that focuses on another problem with one common cause/effect mixup, involving a common misuse of the word "when".)

I personally am somewhat obsessive about changing the imprecise and technically inaccurate "couple of" to "few" whenever I have the authority to do so. Other editors I know don't mind it so much.

One editor I know hates "towards" in US books and wants the oft-official US version: "toward", while I'm perfectly content to let an author pick which version they want to default to. (Note that if you use "toward" as your default, physical motion can get the "s" added on. So that's a third option that an author can follow.)

Editors aren't the only ones with their taste preferences. Some folks enjoy a movie or a story as a whole, while others enjoy movies or stories for the details.

Consider your average book review that's left on Amazon, which answers "Did you enjoy this story?" A big-picture answer could be "I loved how Joe Blue always made lemonade from his lemons!" or "Suzie Maye was so annoying, but I couldn't help but love her anyway!" A little-picture answer

---

[21] http://blog.janicehardy.com/2012/11/when-are-you-telling-trouble-with-when.html

might be "I loved the poem headings to every chapter" or "That scene where Joe had to fish Suzie Maye from the semi filled with whipped cream made me cry!"

(Note that I pulled those examples out of the ether and have neither read nor written that particular book. Yet.)

Neither "big picture" nor "little picture" enjoyment is better than the other. They're examples of how everyone's different.

It probably doesn't surprise any of you to know that I (a line editor) tend to be a "little picture" person, focused on the trees. Sometimes I'm unable to see the forest for the trees, but we'll return to that issue in a moment.

Sudoku's a breeze for me, and checkers isn't too hard, but chess? Eek. So much to keep track of and analyze! (Interestingly, as I've gotten better at analyzing the "big picture" for stories and my own writing, I've gotten better at chess, too.)

I often intentionally practice stepping back and eyeing the "big picture", like when I'm writing a book review on Goodreads, but it's not easy for me. With practice, I'm getting better, and I'm finding my overall enjoyment of what I read is increasing as a result.

But that doesn't make me able to read a typo-filled first draft and appreciate the underlining "big picture" very well.

Someone who can't see the forest for the trees—or can't see the trees for the forest—in a piece of writing you hand them isn't necessarily being rude. They just might not be the person to ask for the type of input you're seeking. That doesn't mean there's necessarily something wrong with you or them. That just means you need to find someone else to ask when you want the kind of input you're looking for. (If a reader just doesn't know how to address what you want to know, some leading questions can usually help, like "What did you like most?" and "Did my commas look right?")

We're all different, and that's something to keep in mind while writing, editing, and seeking reviews.

What about you? Do you tend to analyze and enjoy things on a "little-picture" level or a "big-picture" level?[22]

---

[22] http://carradee.blogspot.com/2011/12/2-types-of-editors-in-this-world.html

Playing to Your Strengths— Writing to Hide Your Weaknesses

Shortly before I wrote this chapter, similar blog posts went up in a guest post by Red Tash[23] over on David Gaughran's blog[24] and by Bob Mayer[25] on his blog.

So even though I had it planned first, it could come across as being more of a copycat. Ah, well.

Still, those posts speak of making sure the first story or stories you write are simple enough for you to pull off, so Red Tash and Bob Mayer were specifically talking to newer writers. (If you've not read the posts, go ahead and check them out, as well as Jami Gold's post[26] addressing a different tack over on her blog. Worth reading. ^_^ I'll wait.)

Read them? Good. Now, I agree with Red Tash and Bob Mayer's advice, but…

I'm with Jami. I don't believe that making sure you can pull a story off only applies to newer writers.

---

[23] http://davidgaughran.wordpress.com/2011/12/06/guest-post-by-red-tash-should-you-write-your-second-book-first/

[24] http://davidgaughran.wordpress.com/

[25] http://writeitforward.wordpress.com/2011/12/02/what-to-write/

[26] http://jamigold.com/2012/04/do-your-stories-match-your-voice/

I believe that *everyone* should make sure their project of choice is something they can pull off.

Don't get me wrong—if you write as a hobby or a profession, you should always seek to stretch yourself. But if you struggle with organizing logical plots and always have to go back and make sure you didn't overthink something and turn the plot into nonsense or *deus ex machina*? Well... As much as you might long to try your hand at writing cozy mysteries, you probably aren't ready for that, yet. (Yes, I'm talking about myself with that one.)

This is where self-editing comes into play.

Let's say you struggle to put sentences together, and your employer wants you to write a how-to manual. How-to manuals are a specific type of technical writing that require good structure. If you can't structure your content well, then you really shouldn't be writing a how-to manual.

If you're being held responsible for a skill you don't have, it might be time to look for another job.

But if you have options for what you can work on next, start self-editing *before* you plan your next project. Sit down with all your ideas and consider how they fit your abilities. What do you struggle with? What are you *good* at? What will each project require?

Struggle to write realistic dialogue, but your action scenes are killer? Then that character-driven drama with nuanced conversations probably isn't the best choice, right now. But lonely assassin story might fit your current skills.

Do you have a hard time writing distinct voices for your different PoV (Point of View) characters, but your humor scenes can make readers laugh out loud? Then that multigenerational southern gothic one probably won't work, but a lighthearted story limited to one PoV, maybe two, might work well.

Does plotting make you whimper and rip your outline to shreds and go back to the emotional arc outline? Then that plot-heavy spy novel probably won't work, unless you could make it character-oriented… Hmm. That might actually work.

See what I mean?

As I work on flushing out the original blog posts for this book, I have a few other nonfiction projects on the back burner. But they pretty much require either time-intensive research and data compilation, or they require me to plan and write all the text outright. I'm working on this in short spurts, on breaks from my other projects; those other projects will be better to work on when I can devote more time to them per sitting. I'm aware of that and planning accordingly.

Now, don't neglect stretching yourself; but *don't stretch yourself in every area at once*. That way lay frustration.

Get fairly comfortable with what you're doing, *then* experiment.

Writing company memos? Best to make sure you can be concise and professional before you start trying to add personal touches. Same goes for school essays—it's always best to test to make sure you write what the teacher wants, before you start adding personal flourishes that might result in a higher or lower grade, depending on the teacher.

Are you a fiction writer who always writes in third person limited? Try first person or omniscient PoV. Always use present tense? Try past.

If you're feeling *really* adventurous—and are willing to produce something you probably won't be able to sell—try second person PoV or one of the "forbidden" verb tenses (future, present perfect, past perfect). Those things aren't used for a reason, so trying to produce something that works despite that reason can be quite a valuable exercise.

Are your stories always dialogue-heavy? Make yourself write a short story that's description and monologue.

Are your stories always description-heavy? Try writing a flash fiction piece of pure dialogue.

If your experiment flunks, then you aren't as comfortable with your writing as you thought. Keep going. Keep practicing.

But don't tackle too many experiments at once unless you're willing to risk biting off more than you can chew.

For a writer (who writes on purpose) to have novel or story ideas that they can't yet write is *normal*. I have one, myself, that I try to tackle every so often, only to sigh and lament "Not yet." Others that I stir, say "Hmm…", and nudge a little further back on the stove to keep simmering.

And the fun thing is, waiting to tackle the "hard" stuff will make it easier to write once you get to it, because you'll have learned at least some of the things you need, to be able to write it. So when you do sit down and write it, you'll have less to tackle at once.

I struggle with transitions; I don't think with them—which even confuses *me*, sometimes—and therefore have had to study when they're needed. I realized that it would be better for me to focus on stories with a limited timeline. **But—**

Even those limited timelines need transitions at every scene shift. So even in avoiding stories that taxed that problem area, I was practicing the transitions, getting better at using them—and my ability to write a first draft that'll be coherent to someone other than me has increased dramatically.

It's similar in nonfiction. Get used to the baseline for what your audience (be it superiors or clients) wants, *then* improvise. If you don't wait until you understand what they want before you get creative with it, your improvisation might just cut the very thing your audience needs most.

Do you believe all writers need concern themselves about considering their skill set before writing, or that only new writers need do so? Why?[27]

---

[27] http://carradee.blogspot.com/2011/12/playing-to-your-strengths-writing-to.html

EDITING MINDSET

The Sun also Sets—
Writers and Depression

Writers are notoriously prone to depression. Just think of all the big-name authors who have died young, either from suicide or other causes, like abusing their bodies. Ernest Hemingway and several songwriters spring to mind, and that's before I even check the Wikipedia lists[28].

Maybe it's because of all the time we writers spend in our heads, riding our characters' emotions as well as our own. Or maybe it's the historically erratic paychecks and common derision from others who keep telling us to get "real jobs".

Or maybe emotional types are more drawn to writing. Hard to say. I've seen one study that indicated probable correlation between writing and emotional issues, but correlation and causation are two different things.

I don't know about you, but the high incidence of self-abuse and suicide in classic authors scared me, when I was in high school literature classes. Made me wonder if I was doomed to a gloomy life of depression and angst. (Be glad I don't inflict my first few novels on you.)

As I've gotten older, I've realized that I'm prone to (mild) depression, too, and I definitely have PTSD and anxiety issues.

---

[28] http://en.wikipedia.org/wiki/Category:Writers_who_committed_suicide

I make no secret of the detail that I have a hormone disorder. Sometimes, it makes me giddy and inexplicably happy, but more often...

If my laundry lingers unfolded for more than a day, I'm depressed. If it lingers *folded* but not put away... Well, I'd better get some vitamin D a.s.a.p. (Vitamin D's technically not a vitamin; it's a hormone that your body creates out of sunshine exposure. Mine tends to be low. One time I had it checked, it was lower than a few of my doctors had ever seen. I'm literally allergic to the outdoors—grass, trees, shrubs, cacti, flowers... Not kidding or exaggerating.)

That sunlight's often the most effective treatment for depression—for *me*, anyway. Going out for some frozen yogurt or to visit some friends can help...unless neighbors are mowing their lawns, since I then *cannot* go outdoors, thanks to my grass allergy. (Alert: if you take melatonin to help you sleep, that can make depression worse, too.)

Okay. Great. Depression's not unusual for writers. Why am I bringing it up, and how does it relate to self-editing?

First, why I'm bringing this up: Nobody was interested in a giveaway I held in the end of 2011 for my first Darkworld novel, *Destiny's Kiss*[29].

As depressing as that is, I don't say that as a pity party. I say that to point out: The lack of responses suggests I *did something wrong.*

The giveaway might've been an idea that was better in my head than in practice—or maybe I didn't have a large enough following for a giveaway to work, yet.

---

[29] http://www.amazon.com/gp/product/B0058WC3TG/

No biggie. Live and learn.

Intellectually, I was always fine about that, and that's the part of me that dominates. (Thankfully.) I have some ideas about causes or correlations of that failed giveaway, so I hopefully won't repeat that flunk, next time I try something comparable.

Emotionally, while writing the original post this chapter is built on, I was pointedly distracting myself with songs like "Another Mad Science Love Song" and "Oh, Michelle" by Seanan McGuire[30] when I started dwelling on the "Nobody wanted a *free* story!" aspect. (Fair warning: I'm a fan of black humor.)

I know I can write well, but that doesn't keep my emotions from being ornery. Big deal. I'm used to it.

So I'm aware of the depression, and I'm fighting it—two things that many, many writers have to do regularly. I'm no special cookie in that regard.

There is nothing "wrong" about struggling with depression. It doesn't make you a bad person; and if you're Christian, depression doesn't mean you don't trust God. (I've had pastors say that depression means you don't trust God, as if there aren't other reasons—like, oh *biological* ones—for someone to be depressed.)

Stress can cause depression, too. So it doesn't matter if you love to write or have to write because you're a student or your day job requires it. If you write, you're potentially susceptible to depression.

And that's *normal*.

---

[30] http://seananmcguire.com/

Second: How does writer depression relate to self-editing?

If you have to ask that, you've never faced a "sea of red"—a good editorial pen. (And if you've never given *yourself* a "sea of red," you probably aren't the best at self-editing. Are there exceptions? Yes. Some folks produce very clean first drafts. Are you likely one of them? Not unless you're already a voracious reader and you've already received a sea of red at some point. And even in that case, your "sea of red" will likely pop up somewhere, even if it's in the insertions you make on your second draft. Note that there are exceptions.)

Look, I *work* as an editor, and sometimes as a tutor. And all the less practiced writers I work with are convinced that they're the most terrible writer ever when they see the corrections I make—even when I reassure them that they're not. (I could tell tales of writing so bad that... Never mind.)

The writers who've faced the sea of red before have some sense in how to conquer that "Oh, I *suck*!" sensation that comes when you're looking at a piece that needs fixing. Some have even learned to love the sea of red, viewing it as the learning opportunity it's supposed to be.

Because not everything needs outright revision or rewriting.

It's like my high fantasy novel *A Fistful of Fire*[31]. I mercilessly marked up a printed copy of the book, then realized when putting in the edits that most of the changes were downright *optional*. Which I noticed because I'd bothered to take a step back and to take a deep breath before I dove into making the corrections.

---

[31] http://www.amazon.com/gp/product/B004UMG1PC/

If I'd been depressed, I would've applied every little change, some of which would've altered parts of the story into the voice of the narrator of my dark urban fantasy novel *Destiny's Kiss*[32]. (…Oops?)

When you're writing, when you're editing—whether it's self-editing or with a beta reader or with a paid editor—you need to pay attention to your personal cues. You should have something that you can pay attention to, to notice when you're getting depressed. Being aware of those signals can enable you to nip that depression in the bud.

The sun does set.

But remember that it rises, too.

What cues you in when you're getting depressed? Do you notice? How do you counter the feeling?[33]

---

[32] http://www.amazon.com/gp/product/B0058WC3TG/
[33] http://carradee.blogspot.com/2011/12/sun-also-setswriters-and-depression.html

EAT THAT ELEPHANT:
EDIT EFFECTIVELY

Okay, so I stole the analogy from Kristine Kathryn Rusch[34] and Dean Wesley Smith[35], but I don't think they'll mind. "Eat that elephant" comes from a question: "How do you eat an elephant?"

Let's say you have a cooked elephant in front of you and must eat it. (Maybe it's the only food you'll get until you finish it, or some despot will take your head off if you don't, or maybe you have your own preferred reason behind having to eat it.)

If you look at the elephant carcass, you'll get overwhelmed. You'll think—no, you'll *know*—that it'll take forever to eat and God only knows when you'll finish it.

And while you dither over how gargantuan your elephant is and how impossible it is for *anyone* to eat, your neighbor is quietly finishing theirs.

It's the basic concept of breaking things down into manageable chunks. If you look at too much at once, you'll be overwhelmed and the task will take far longer than necessary. (Yes, I omitted that comma before the conjunction on purpose,

---

[34] http://kriswrites.com/
[35] http://deanwesleysmith.com/

so the "if you look at too much at once" would apply to both clauses.)

So how do you eat an elephant? **One bite at a time.**

Different folks have different-sized mouths, too, so chunks that are "bite-sized" for one person might choke someone else. The issue is knowing yourself and how much you can handle at a time. You also need to be flexible when something happens that sabotages what you can handle, bending with the problems rather than breaking under them.

You might be asking, "What does project planning have to do with editing effectively?"

Everything.

While writing the blog post that formed the basis for this chapter, I had several writing projects on the to-do list.

- A novelette to finish writing for an upcoming deadline. (And now while I put this book together, I don't even remember what project that was, to know if I managed it or not.)

- A final ten thousand words or so to write in *A Fistful of Earth*[36], the sequel to *A Fistful of Fire*[37], which then needed a heavy coherence edit, because some major things changed while I was working on the story, but I didn't go back to make it all fit. (That edit took a lot longer than expected, but it's done.)

---

[36] http://www.amazon.com/gp/product/B009Z54Y8U/
[37] http://www.amazon.com/gp/product/B004UMG1PC/

- And Jami Gold[38] was hosting a pitch session on her blog that I'd thought a particular novelette of mine would fit well—if I could finish it a week after the other deadline. (I finished it, mulled over expanding it into a novel, released it in novelette form. I later released the sequel novella and am now working on #3 in the series.)

- Oh, and I got asked by an anthology for a story. No deadline, but I wanted to be prompt about submitting something. (I was. It was accepted.)

And remember, my day job is writing, editing, and proofreading for clients. So it's easy to get overwhelmed, to go "Ulgh! I've already edited twenty thousand words today! I'm done!"

Editing is insidious. It has a way of taking longer than you planned—and of making you think that's okay.

Taking longer than planned *is* okay, if the extra time is because the writing needs it.

Taking longer than planned is **not** okay, if the extra time is because you're letting the size of the task ahead of you overwhelm you and slow you down.

When it's genuinely a lot of work ahead of you, you'll probably take longer than expected. That's fine. But taking longer than expected because you're dithering over what to do and feeling overwhelmed? Not fine.

See the difference?

To edit effectively, you break your task down into chunks. Get it done one bite at a time.

---

[38] http://jamigold.com/2011/12/write-fiction-why-you-should-try-a-short-story/

That might mean one type of editing at a time. That might mean one paragraph or chapter at a time. That might mean one task at a time—like reading through to evaluate what it needs, then making the plot connect, then the characters, etc.

It all depends on *you*, how *you* think, work, write. On how much practice you have, on how comfortable you are with different types of editing.

And different pieces of writing will need different things.

For example, this book is nonfiction. I've included appendixes and frequent links to the original blog posts that these chapters were based on. While I theoretically could've done something similar in *A Fistful of Fire*[39], for example, (which was originally serialized on a blog), those questions and links to join the comments wouldn't have fit fiction.

If you're writing a college essay, you need an introductory paragraph and a concluding paragraph. In a professional e-mail or a letter, you often need the same thing—or at least the appropriate salutation and signature for your audience.

Checklists can be your friend, here, to make sure you have all the necessary pieces. Consider what you're writing, make a quick checklist about what the structural parts of it are, then check them off the list.

I often edit as I go. But when I get stumped and can't figure out structural issues on the fly, I like breaking it down with Holly Lisle[40]'s notecard method, except instead of colored notecards, I use white ones. Then I color-code the top edge to indicate if a scene's good, needs some work, needs a lot of work, or needs tossing. (I'll describe this process further in a later chapter.)

---

[39] http://www.amazon.com/gp/product/B004UMG1PC/
[40] http://hollylisle.com/

But this is *me*, how *I* work. Not everybody can write content and critically evaluate it at the same time—and even then, I draft faster if I drop the critical mode, getting a possible fifteen hundred words or more words per hour. (Depends on the narrator.)

Even if I do that, I have to then stop and clean up the drafted bit before I can continue. I often pull off an "average" pace of one thousand words (or more) per hour with critical mode on, so I usually find it easier to just edit as I go. I don't get interrupted as much.

Not everybody's comfortable tackling content edits, line edits, copyedits, and proofreading at the selfsame time. Even though I'm practiced at it, *I'm* not comfortable with it. When I start getting overwhelmed, I make sure to break it up a.s.a.p., so I don't waste too much time dithering over how much I have to do. (*A Fistful of Earth*[41] needed such breaking down. That thing was a *mess*.)

How do you usually break down your editing?[42]

---

[41] http://www.amazon.com/gp/product/B009Z54Y8U/

[42] http://carradee.blogspot.com/2011/12/eat-that-elephant-edit-effectively.html

SELF-EDITING
AND SELF-EVALUATION

It's been said, many a time, that artists (and writers) are their own worst critics.

We know what we meant to put on the canvas (page), the effect it's *supposed* to have. Did it work? Did it not?

We're said to be too close to our work to know.

This is why writers rely on beta readers or critique groups. Rip it apart, spit it out, say what works, say what doesn't.

(Note: Some professional authors and editors with a whole lot more experience than I do insist that the only critique that really matters among pros is whether you liked it or not. Note, though, that the folks who say that assume you are competent in basic structure, grammar, and storytelling.)

I've heard it said that writers *can't* evaluate their own work, but I'm unconvinced. Often, I've noticed that when I'm *unsure* about something, betas really like it.

But when I'm *certain* something doesn't work? Betas agree with me.

And those writers I edit? If a client says "I think there's something wrong with the structure," well, there's something wrong (or at least unusual) about the structure.

(I don't go into a work expecting to find those problems, either. I actually forget the author said anything—if they said anything—until I start noticing the problem. Then I think, "Hope the author's okay with hearing there's structure problem—oh, right. They said they was worried about that." That or I'll remember the author's concern just as I'm falling asleep the night after I've finished the edit. My memory's weird like that.)

Now, as a **writer**, when I'm nervous or unsure about something, I've found it's usually best to leave it alone.

But when there's certainty? Fix it.

Sure, there are exceptions. At one point, I thought *A Fistful of Fire*[43] needed a complete overhaul to fit more conventional plot structure, but then I realized that would damage the story. (It also helped that I read *Summers at Castle Auburn*[44] by Sharon Shinn[45], which was the closest thing I'd found to certain things I was trying to do in *A Fistful of Fire*[46].)

I dove into *Summers at Castle Auburn*[47] expecting a political fantasy. I found a sweet fantasy romance with some mystery/intrigue woven in. I can't remember if the book was a gift from a friend or something I picked up at a secondhand shop. Probably the latter—my friends tend to avoid buying me books because they know that anything they're familiar with is likely to be a duplicate on my bookshelf. That or they know that I don't have bookshelf space. One or the other—couldn't possibly be a mixture of both. ^_^

---

[43] http://www.amazon.com/gp/product/B004UMG1PC/
[44] http://www.amazon.com/gp/product/B000OCXG32/
[45] http://sharonshinn.net/HTML/index_HTML.html
[46] http://www.amazon.com/gp/product/B004UMG1PC/
[47] http://www.amazon.com/gp/product/B000OCXG32/

That book helped me recognize that *A Fistful of Fire* was what I'd wanted it to be, so I let it go. Reader comments since I released it have confirmed that it's what I intended.

The efficacy of a self-evaluation also differs from author to author, and likely even from story to story.

But with practice—and that means practice evaluating *new* stories, not the selfsame one over and over—I do believe that a writer or an artist can get better at identifying when there's a specific problem with their work. I even believe that a person can get better and identifying where a problem is.

So how *does* a writer evaluate their own work? First you take your drafted piece, give it a hard look, identify what effect you think the different parts of it have...

Then you hand it off to a trusted beta reader (or a coworker, or a teacher), someone prone to spotting the type of issue you think is there, to see if the story did what you wanted.

If it failed, you can try again; or, if the story works but it isn't what you wanted, you can accept the story for what it is.

If it succeeded, you can rejoice and hope the next one will do the same.

And while you're working on that in your own writing, you quietly work on evaluating others' stories that you read, as well. When you love a book, see if you can track down some specifics that you think made you love it. If a book's lost your interest, you needn't force yourself to read through it, but see if you can identify what made you lose interest.

Personally, I like reading popular books that I don't particularly care for, to see about identifying what those authors did right.

Because if an author hits it big, *they did something right*. All the jealousy or typographical errors or bad research or superfluous adverbs doesn't negate that the author did something right, something you could potentially learn.

Once you have some ideas about examples of things done *right*, pick one. *One*. See if you can produce that effect in your own writing.

Did you catch that I'm talking about attempting to imitate *one* effect at a time, here?

And your beta reader—who should be someone who likes that thing you're trying to pull off—gets to tell you if you succeeded or not.

Those times you miss your goal, try again. Usually, trying again with a *new* story will be best.

But if you find yourself completely rewriting *every* little word and phrase because you're certain it isn't good enough, **stop**. There's something called over-editing, and the results ain't pretty.

Little makes me sadder than reading something that's had all the life edited out of it, evidenced by hints of an effective creative description or turn of phrase that peek through. I usually don't know if it's the author, their beta readers, or some "professional" editors responsible for the over-editing, but it makes me sad, all the same.

Writers need to have some confidence in what they write— enough to catch when something just didn't click with a beta reader or editor, but not so much that they miss when a beta reader or editor has a legitimate complaint.

In example, notice the prepositional phrase I just used to start this sentence. Technically, "in example" makes sense, and you can get my gist—but that isn't the standard phrasing. The usual is "for example" or "as an example", so "in example" reads as an error or as unnecessarily emphatic, rather than as a useful creative phrasing.

Note that I am **not** saying an author can accurately evaluate the *quality* of something they write. I'm saying an author **might** be able to accurately evaluate the major *problems* in a piece they write.

We can't judge our own quality, because we either see or overlook every flaw, real and imagined.

But maybe we can judge when our intended comedy story might've ended up with a despicable heroine.

And in doing so, we can at least have some idea of what kind of help we need to fix it…assuming it's fixable, or that we even want to fix it.

Do you find that your self-evaluation of story errors matches what your beta tells you? Or, if you're a beta reader, do you find that the writer(s) you beta read can accurately judge the errors in their own work?[48]

---

[48] http://carradee.blogspot.com/2012/01/self-editing-and-self-evaluation.html

WHY GOOD SELF-EDITING IS (NOT?) "IMPOSSIBLE"

Hearkening back to my first chapter in this book, "Is Self-Editing Unprofessional?", I pointed out the dichotomy about self-editing. While there's a common belief in self-publishing (and even among fiction authors) that it's *impossible* for an author to adequately edit their own work, freelance writers (and some traditionally published writers) are *expected* to be able to adequately edit their own work.

But a lot of writers—employees, students, authors—think that adequately self-editing their own work is impossible. That isn't necessarily true, but it *can* be true, due to what's involved.

See, "Editing" involves several tasks that not everyone can do, never mind well, and it's normal to be able to analyze problems in someone else's writing before you can analyze them in your own writing. Definitions also change a bit depending on the situation and who you ask, so I'll define what I mean:

- **Content Editing** – Making sure the "big picture" works—your content, definitions, arguments, information, plot, characters, setting, theme, etc.

- **Line Editing** – Making sure each sentence flows in the best way possible.

- **Copyediting** – Making sure the text says what you wanted it to say, that the details line up, and that your references and such are done properly.

- **Proofreading** – A final check for misused words, misplaced punctuation, improper formatting, etc.

So when you self-edit, you have to make sure your "big picture" structure all works—and that the structure matches what you're writing—*and* you have to make sure you didn't use the noun *affect* where you needed the noun *effect*, or that you didn't use the female *fiancée* where you needed the male *fiancé*. (Two examples of common problems. And yes, *affect* can be a noun, though it's usually used as a verb.)

When you self-edit, you have to do all those things by yourself.

…Or do you?

Something that a lot of folks forget or scoff at when they insist *nobody* can self-edit: beta readers.

Beta readers likely aren't pros (because pros usually want a hobby that doesn't involve them continuing the day job in their spare time). Beta readers probably don't know when a semicolon should go before a conjunction. (Yes, it sometimes should, or at least can, go there.) Beta readers might not be particularly familiar with your genre but want to read it because you wrote it.

But beta readers are *readers*. I have friends who work or have worked as English teachers, as staff proofreaders for an extremely picky press, etc. And some of my best feedback, the input that nailed the problem in a story's content, does *not* come from them.

I repeat: My most useful content feedback often comes from my friends who do **not** work in the field.

Detail input? Analysis of story theme? Debate about if a technique I tried was appropriate to the context? My professional friends are fantastic at that.

For example, one of them critiqued an early version of *A Fistful of Fire*[49]. Her "Mash doesn't boil!" sounded like my complaint about Robin McKinley's *Sunshine*[50]: "Knitting needles don't have hooks on the end!" See, the book mentioned a long needle that "even" had a hook on the end. Knitting needles don't really have hooks. I've since heard that some do, but McKinley's description makes me see an afghan hook, also known as a Tunisian crochet hook. (I even suspect the author wrote that on purpose due to the narrator, but it still irritates me.)

Ahem.

My non-professional friends are the ones who told me my paranoid narrator for *A Fistful of Fire*[51] was *too* whiny and self-absorbed (who I then toned down for the final version).

The non-professionals pointed out that I was getting extremely rude and snappish, when I tried writing a novel full of psychopaths for National Novel Writing Month[52]. (It put me on edge, and they later told me that just hearing about the story sorta scared them. I've learned that I can't bury myself in that

---

[49] http://www.amazon.com/gp/product/B004UMG1PC/
[50] http://www.amazon.com/gp/product/0515138819/
[51] http://www.amazon.com/gp/product/B004UMG1PC/
[52] http://nanowrimo.org/

kind of story again; it isn't healthy. Short spurts are fine; long ones, no.)

The non-professionals can help ensure that you don't get lost in the writing, that you don't hurt yourself, and that you have a life outside all the fun in your head.

Beta readers can help you fill in your editing weak points, but even then, you have to be skilled enough as a self-editor to know where your weak points are and to recognize when a beta reader's suggestion is legitimate. I've had friends try copyediting or proofreading my work, where I then discovered that they didn't know grammar quite as thoroughly as they thought they did, or that they used a different grammar handbook and dictionary than I did.

Differing grammar handbooks and dictionaries can make the difference between putting spaces around an em dash (—) or not, and between the spelling of words like *e-mail/email*. (For the record, I prefer no spaces and *e-mail*.)

So, before you can self-edit or pick good support beta readers, you already need some skill at editing.

You need some skill at *all* types of editing.

That's a lot of work. It's scary. Some folks don't want to spend the time to learn it thoroughly, time that could be spent writing. That's *fine*.

I repeat: Folks who like to write do not *need* to learn how to adequately self-edit. They'll have to find people willing to put up with the same errors time after time, with no improvement—but such people can be hired if you don't have any capable and willing fans, eager to volunteer. (I don't say that to be snarky. I point it out as a legitimate option.)

Some folks have learning disabilities or issues that mean they honestly *can't* adequately edit their own work. That's fine, too. (Though such people can probably learn more than they think they can; speaking from my experience as a grammar tutor, here.)

But self-editing **is not impossible** for everyone. Just ask a student who's aced a timed school essay, or a freelancer who's worked under an NDA with no more than an *acquisitions* editor.

Do you seek to improve your self-editing skills, or do you focus on your writing? If you're more of a reader than a writer, what errors particularly bother you in a story?[53]

---

[53] http://carradee.blogspot.com/2012/01/why-good-self-editing-is-not-impossible.html

Tricks Instead of Treats: Tricking Yourself

We've covered topics like how self-editing isn't innately "unprofessional", why it's difficult to edit your own work, and how to avoid the worst of your writing problems.

Now, to get into some of the nitty-gritty of how exactly this self-editing thing works: You must trick yourself.

Can you trick yourself?

If you can't, your first step in self-editing will have to be figuring out how. (Don't fret over it, at this point. There are many possible tactics you can try, and I'll be mentioning several in later chapters. Knowing your learning style can help, but it isn't mandatory.)

When you read something you've written, you see what you *meant* to do—the "treats," as it were. To edit and revise it appropriately, you must trick yourself into seeing what's actually there.

Not what you *think* is there. You have to see what's actually on the page.

And since you know exactly what you *intended* to say, that's a whole lot harder to do for yourself than it is to do for someone else. (Thus why it's normal for someone to be able to critique others' writing but to miss the selfsame mistakes in their own writing.)

On a copyediting and proofreading level, there are several options available for tricking yourself. All of them are tedious, but they work pretty well, particularly when you combine methods. (I'll share specific methods later.)

Not that tricking yourself to see what's actually on the page will do you much good if you don't know how to copyedit or proofread (or if you're particularly dyslexic), but I'm going to assume that you're honest with yourself when you evaluate your ability.

(Side note: If you can't edit and can't afford an editor, have you checked out the possibilities of bartering or crowdsourcing[54]? I'm assuming you aren't a college student whose university considers editing help to be cheating.)

With big-picture editing, however, tricking ourselves is a bit harder. We have to see the arguments and scenes and plots as they **actually** fit together, not how we *want* or *meant* them to fit together.

For doing this, some writers use note cards, one per section (topic, scene, etc.), then organize those cards for each of the different things they're checking and take notes about what needs fixing.

Nonfiction example: An essay could have note cards for each point that can or must be made in support of your arguments for a thesis. The note cards could be marked with the necessary points that absolutely must be in your essay (such as "I must use all these academic journal references, because the essay must have a minimum of three, and that's how many I found"). You can also arrange the note cards to see how many

---

[54] http://en.wikipedia.org/wiki/Crowdsourcing

supporting points you have for each argument supporting your thesis, to evaluate that the strength of your supporting arguments. (This is good for helping you find your weakest arguments, which can be bolstered to add words or removed to cut words from your paper—whichever you need.)

Personally, when I was writing essays in college, I would jot down all the basic points I had that related to my topic in a bullet list. That gave me enough to quickly figure out the basic structure for the essay.

Fiction example: A story with multiple PoVs could have note cards arranged for the author to see how many scenes they have, for each PoV, and to figure out how they want to arrange those scenes. The author could also then rearrange them to see how many cards dealt with a particular, say, romance subplot, and where those scenes fell, to make sure they were spaced throughout the story.

Bullet lists can be used for these things, too, but bullet lists tend to work best for short, simple lists rather than long or complicated ones.

If you have the program Scrivener[55], you can set keywords on each scene, and then run different searches to check the items. (Other programs might also have the keyword function, but I don't know about them.)

---

[55] http://www.literatureandlatte.com/scrivener.php

Some writers just take a notebook and read through the manuscript multiple times, checking different aspects each time.

Some folks do a single read-through and leave it, but the ones who pull that off tend to have more experience reading and writing whatever they're working on.

In their school years, most folks learn to write conventional, numbered sentence outlines for essays. That's one method, a popular one for nonfiction, though it isn't necessarily helpful. (This method actually made essays extremely difficult for me to write. My grades were always better without them.)

Though Scrivener's keywords can be incredibly handy for making sure a minor character didn't mysteriously vanish for half the book, I generally do my scene-by-scene analysis by either plugging my story into some *Save the Cat!*[56]–type beat sheets, set up in a spreadsheet, or by with physical 3x5 note cards. I use a variant of methods I've read from…Holly Lisle[57] and Shanna Swendson[58], if I rightly recall my sources correctly.

The most unique detail about how I modify others' techniques is how I color them. Holly Lisle uses colored note cards to indicate how much work a scene needs (green for next to none, red for scrap and redo, etc). Instead, I put all my scenes down on white cards, then take highlighters or markers and mark along the top edge of the card. (So when you take the stack, flip it so the text is facing you for you to read, and the

---

[56] http://www.amazon.com/gp/product/B00340ESIS/
[57] http://hollylisle.com/
[58] http://shannaswendson.com/

color shows on top of the stack.) I also make a "Key" card, with the story title, the colors, and what those colors mean.

(Reason for avoiding color with the actual text: Thanks to a quirk of my specific unusual learning style, color hinders me, so limiting the color to the top of the card keeps the color from getting in my way. My method also allows me to jot down all the scenes, *then* to make the evaluation.)

Afterwards, for organization, I might punch a hole in the corner of every card and misshape a paper clip to use as a ring. More often, I take a small check envelope and write the book title on it, then stick the note cards inside.

Whatever technique you use to break down your writing into chunks to see what's supposed to be there, pick what works for you.

I'm being intentionally vague here about *what* to check, because that'll differ depending on your type of story and how you write it, but I'll share some ideas about that later.

Knowing what to check will do you little good if you have no idea how to tackle it.

Can you trick yourself into seeing what's actually on the page rather than what you want to be there? How do you do it?[59]

---

[59] http://carradee.blogspot.com/2012/01/tricks-instead-of-treats-tricking.html

(SELF-)EDITING AND EFFICIENCY

Is it possible to edit yourself *efficiently*?

Yes, in the sense that you can make use of different self-editing methods to speed yourself up.

By *efficiently*, I mean that you can self-edit, producing a quality product in the least amount of time possible for yourself.

Some commenters on the blog posts for this series have mentioned that they use the "Let it sit" technique. They leave their writing for a time before they come back to it to edit.

While that's a good one, that technique caters to letting you do whichever type of editing you're best at: big picture or little picture. (Remember my chapter on the two main types of editors?) Letting your writing sit doesn't necessarily do you the most good for whichever type of editing you're not so good at.

All stories need a "big picture" check and a "little picture" check. What those checks look like, though, will vary from writer to writer, and different writers will do those checks at different points in the writing process.

Some folks spew words on paper and check both afterwards. Some labor over an outline to make sure the overarching story will even work before they start the prose. Some edit and "outline" (in that they make general notes, not an actual outline) as they write the story (*raises hand*).

Here's the thing: On a purely objective level, you might expect it to be *most* efficient to start out outlining (to check the big picture), spewing everything out on the page (because you can't fix what's not on the page—well, sort of), and then polishing everything up.

But everyone's wired differently. That plan-first method is only efficient for **some** people.

Some folks, those of us who are naturally best at spotting the "little picture," actually work best by cleaning up the "little picture" first, because even if that means we "waste" time polishing text that'll be tossed, it saves time by making us able to see beyond the misused commas to fully process the content beneath.

Can such a "little picture" editor get better at seeing the content beneath the grammar errors? Yes. But that requires the "little picture" editor to practice "big picture" editing, so it becomes more natural.

Hey, I've never said this learning to self-edit thing was easy or quick.

So the most efficient editing method **for you** might not be be what you'd expect to be efficient.

Personal example: It's impossible for me to use an outline as a fluid structural guideline.

Folks talk about using the outline as a rough idea, something to be changed as the story goes, but it is pretty much **impossible** for me to rearrange a standard alphanumeric outline, even when it's on the computer screen.

The reason? As soon as everything's organized with numbers and letters, *I cannot visualize it any other way*. It's like permanent brain freeze.

It gave me a ton of trouble in school when teachers would demand I provide one of those alphanumeric outlines before I wrote a paper, all topic sentences in place. I can sometimes adjust a topical outline a little, but a *sentence* outline? Forget it.

Let's just say I learned to write the paper's rough draft before I wrote the outline. *twiddles thumbs* Most teachers who found out weren't happy about it, so I learned to keep my mouth shut.

So, for classes where my grade would've been docked if I'd written the paper first, I would create and reorganize a bulleted list. If I had time, I'd write the paper and then write the outline in time to turn it in, but when that wasn't an option, I'd modify the bullet list into an alphanumeric outline to turn in to the teacher, looking at that outline for as short a time as possible.

I suspect it's my learning style. Most visual learners are polychromatic from pictures. In other words, color, pictures, and their own handwriting all help them.

I'm monochromatic from typed words. In other words, I struggle to read handwriting (even my own), a good way to get me to *not* notice something is to highlight it and not tell me there's color on the page, and pictures are difficult for me to process. (Then again, my lack of depth perception might contribute to that last one.) If I don't think to check for anything other than black text on a white background, I actually won't see that alternatively-colored text.

I include that personal story as a case in point: Alphanumeric sentence outlines are efficient for *some* people. Not everyone.

So when you approach self-editing (or even editing in general), remember: What's efficient for *you* might not be intuitive, or even what's efficient for whatever author(s) you personally look up to.

A method's failure to work for *you* doesn't mean there's anything wrong with either the method or you. It just makes you different.

And differences are a good thing. That's what makes one of us pick up *Lord of the Rings* and think it the quintessential example of fantasy at its finest—and another of us think it a fantastic example of everything boring in the heroic fantasy genre.

Do you have any fun personal stories about an "efficient" technique being incredibly inefficient for you? Care to share?[60]

---

[60] http://carradee.blogspot.com/2012/01/self-editing-and-efficiency.html

A Caveat about Self-Editing

Editing comes in multiple types, and the definitions about those types will differ depending on whom you ask, but something needs to be borne in mind when self-editing:

WRITERS CANNOT JUDGE THEIR OWN LEVEL OF EFFECTIVENESS.

This is true for college essays, short stories, magazine articles, ad copy—all of it. (I know I've mentioned this before, but this wasn't the primary focus of that chapter, and I want to be clear.)

Writers know what effects they *intend* to have on the reader. Those intentions affect how writers perceive their own writing.

So while I do believe that some writers can often accurately identify *when* a piece is effective, and that some writers can identify *what prevents* a piece from being effective, I do **not** believe that writers can trust themselves to identify *how* effective a piece of writing is.

- **Possible to answer (sometimes):** Is this item I wrote effective?

- **Impossible to answer:** How effective is this item I wrote?

The first reason for that is simple: **People differ from one another.** That applies to writers and readers both. What one reader finds effective, another won't.

Even a writer who can skillfully portray multiple types of people is still one person, themselves, and they'll see the story through the lens of what they *meant* to say.

That's why it's important for a writer to have betas or trusted "first readers"—one or more persons whose judgment the writer trusts, readers willing to read a writer's stuff and tell them if it works or not. (Or to tell the writer *how* their writing works for that reader. All of us sometimes come up with things that convey completely the wrong moods from what we intended.

Personal example: One line got cut from *Destiny's Kiss*[61] that accidentally made Ambrogino sound too much like a creepy stalker—and if you've read that book... Well. Those characters have enough personal issues without tossing *that* in the pie.

So if you try self-editing, bear in mind that you still will want at least one set of critical eyes going over your manuscript.

Some writers work best by only having one person be that reader—and some of those want only a response of "This works" or "This doesn't work." Others work fine with multiple betas, though betas will often give contradictory advice.

Personally, I find it particularly useful to have a manuscript read by someone *outside* my personal demographic (be it in age, gender, or religious affiliation), because my demographic affects my perspective. A reader who disagrees with me about

---

[61] http://www.amazon.com/gp/product/B0058WC3TG/

life, the universe, and everything, will be inclined to catch situations where I'm missing pertinent transitions.

For example, I discovered that many folks assume that an intimate relationship between first cousins is *necessarily* incest, not knowing that it's allowable per many municipalities and even by the book of Leviticus in the Christian Bible.

There's no line addressing that legality in my short story "The Corpse Cat"[62], which features a set of first cousins who also happen to be lovers. If I'd realized what a hang-up it would be for some readers, I would've sought a place where I could insert a brief explanation. As things stand, the novel wherein those characters reappear has a reference to it being legal.

I'd *thought* I handled the relationship well in "The Corpse Cat"[63]. And per my first readers, I had—but **not** *for folks for whom it's taboo.*

I'd entirely forgotten that first cousin relationships *were* taboo for many people. I've been used to the concept for some years, starting from when I discovered that some of the folks I knew were married first cousins.

If I'd bothered to send that story through a first reader who didn't match my demographic—which was "people who know first cousin relationships can be legal"—I would've known that *before* publication, and I could've addressed the issue.

The story's failure to address those things doesn't necessarily make it flawed, but it does make the story less palatable than it could've been for some readers.

---

[62] http://www.amazon.com/gp/product/B0054GQBLM/
[63] http://www.amazon.com/gp/product/B0054GQBLM/

Do you use one or more beta readers? Have you had situations where someone read your piece and got a completely different message from it than what you intended?[64]

Self-Editing
and the Rule of Two

Have you heard of the rule of two, that it's best to keep no more than two items of the same type beside each other? When I first wrote the blog post for this chapter, Jami Gold[65] had recently reminded me about it.

THE RULE OF TWO:

If you have more than two items of the same type in a row in your story—be it description, dialogue, explanation/exposition*, paragraph structures, sentence structures, or some other "little picture" item—your balance is skewed and may be strengthened by bringing it back on-center, working in variety to increase the depth.

When you find violations of the rule of two, you don't *necessarily* need to do anything. It's a rule *of thumb*, remember? All it does is point out that you're heavy on one type of story element. Your genre, style, and story may suit that particular weight.

This rule of thumb just helps you ensure that, when you are off-balance, it's intentional rather than accidental.

---

[65] http://jamigold.com/2012/02/can-we-have-too-much-voice/

(Some phrase this guideline as "rule of three": "Three items of the same type in a row is probably too many", but I find it less confusing to use the "rule of two" version.)

Anyway, like all rules of writing, this is a rule *of thumb* and only a guideline to help you as a writer. It works everything, fiction and nonfiction alike.

The goal of any type of writing is to keep things 1. clear and 2. interesting for the reader.

And the "rule of two" applies to everything from sentence structure to paragraph function.

In nonfiction, "paragraph functions" are things like definition, opinion, explanation, and quotation. In fiction, paragraph functions are things like dialogue, narrative, action, exposition, thoughts, and backstory.

So, have you a block quote three paragraphs (or sentences) long in your essay? Does the quote truly need to be that long? The answer *might* be yes, but it probably isn't.

Do you have more than two paragraphs of pure dialogue in a row? There should probably be some action or PoV emotion in there. *Maybe* not, but probably.

Some genres and audiences can go beyond the rule of two for particular types of paragraphs. High fantasy, for example, can be heavier on the description and exposition, while a thriller might go above and beyond on the backstory.

The rule of two is simple. Applying it, though, can be a bit more difficult.

FIRST, YOU HAVE TO KNOW WHAT YOUR INTENDED AUDIENCE WILL EXPECT AND ACCEPT.

In fiction, if you have three paragraphs of description in a row, you're heavy on the description. Some would call this an info-dump. That bit of text might be strengthened by working something else in there, to make the balance more even. But if you're writing something where description and exposition are *supposed* to be heavy, then you're fine. (There is good reason Jacqueline Carey[66] used a writing style her Kushiel series that was florid without being purple[67].)

Or if you have three talking heads[68] (lines of dialogue without any description or action around it) in a row, it's a flag that you likely need more setting or action in the scene. (Characters' surroundings and habits should usually affect dialogue.)

In nonfiction, you have to consider what your reader(s) will expect when figuring out how to balance facts with opinion, direct quotes with paraphrasing. A college essay might more frequently use direct quotes (in the US) or paraphrasing (in the UK), and it'll usually be less interested in writer opinions than, for example, an op-ed for a magazine.

SECOND, YOU HAVE TO BE ABLE TO SEE THE DIFFERENT PARAGRAPH TYPES.

Some folks eyeball it. Others use different-colored highlighters to mark every sentence according to what it is. (This highlighted copy might be a print copy, or it might be a

---

[66] http://www.jacquelinecarey.com

[67] http://blog.janicehardy.com/2010/09/rose-by-any-other-name-is-still-too.html

[68] http://blog.janicehardy.com/2009/06/tag-youre-it.html

draft that's in their word processor, taking advantage of the highlighter function.)

Most likely, you'll have some type(s) of paragraphs that you're prone to overusing, and others you're prone to underusing. The PoV you write in can influence this, to the point that your habits might differ depending on your story's narrator or PoV.

But you can help yourself write more balanced text. The most efficient method I've found for me?

I make myself write a short story in the opposite extreme from what I've been writing. (This method might be overkill or too extreme for some writers. I thrive on experimentation and change, to the point that I even have to change up where I sleep. Consistency makes me anxious, for reasons that are off-topic.)

I'm often prone to writing text that's heavy on the dialogue and light on the setting. (If you think *A Fistful of Fire*[69] is light on the description, you should see the original version.) When I realized that, I made myself write a short story that's almost all monologue and description.

That short story's actually how I got started writing scripts, since I was struggling with one aspect of it and my English professor at the time said I'd combined short story and playwriting techniques. I had no clue how to write a play, so I signed up for the playwriting class, the following term. I thereby discovered I'm pretty good at them, when I force myself to think in the mindset required for it. (I'm unused to it, so it's not exactly easy. Once I'm in the mindset, though, I'm fine.)

---

[69] http://www.amazon.com/gp/product/B004UMG1PC/

Writing a short story or flash fiction piece in the opposite extreme does a world of good. I'm actually due to write another one, for practice.

What I find most amusing about those writing exercises? Sometimes you can even sell them. I've had more than one catch the eye of an unbiased third party. *wink*

> *Do you use the rule of two or some other rule of thumb when looking at your writing? Can you think of genre-specific exceptions to the rule of two?*

[70]*   Explanation and exposition are often best avoided in fiction, except in situations like the Sherlock Holmes mysteries, where the explanation is necessary so the reader understands what happened. Even then, be careful not to overdo it.

---

[70]   http://carradee.blogspot.com/2012/03/self-editing-and-rule-of-two.html

EDITING STAGES

ORIENT YOUR MUSE:
EDIT BEFORE YOU WRITE

If you're any kind of writing perfectionist, someone's helpfully chimed "You can't fix what's not on the paper." I might even be the one who said it to you.

And it's true: You can't fix prose that's not on the page.

But if your story idea is going in completely the wrong direction, wouldn't it be nice to figure that out *before* you spend those weeks writing it?

Thought so.

I had a particularly hard time when I tried to start writing *A Fistful of Earth*[71]. (That one gave me about every type of trouble you can imagine.) I couldn't figure out why it felt like such a mass of… *mush*, when I thought about it.

So I tried the method of writing the blurb before I wrote the story, which helped me get started. Problem is, *A Fistful of Earth*[72] has three major events going on, and I had to figure out which one the story was really *about*: the political problems, the family problems, or the love story.

Yes, it's still all three, but writing the blurb helped me untangle which were the actual *story*, which were only what the narrator *thought* was going on, and which are the *backstory*

---

[71] http://www.amazon.com/gp/product/B009Z54Y8U/
[72] http://www.amazon.com/gp/product/B009Z54Y8U/

that'll be influencing further events in the series. (That comment will—or at least should—make sense if you read the series.)

Now, **no two writers are exactly alike**. But sometimes, everyone can benefit from a little story analysis before they sit down to write that story (or research paper).

The question is, what are your particular strengths and weaknesses as a writer, and what methods work for checking your weak spots?

And because we're all different, there is no one answer to that question.

So. What techniques can a writer use to make sure a story's ready to be written? (Note: If I refer to story planning, I'm referring to all possible methods: sentence outlines, topical outlines, numbered outlines, bullet outlines, cork board plans, note card plans, spreadsheets, mind maps, snowflakes, etc.)

1. **The gut check**: Does the story excite you? No? That's a major problem sign, right there, even if the problem is that you fear you'll screw up that idea. Figure out why the story doesn't excite you and decide if it's worth addressing or if you should write something else. If the problem is that you fear your Great-Aunt Sarah reading it, you can decide 1. to get over the fear, 2. to use a private alter ego (penname), or 3. to write another story—but you can't make that decision until you identify what's hindering you.

2. **The elevator pitch**: Figure out the "elevator pitch" for your story or book: one sentence that sums it up. As of early 2015, Jami Gold really has

the definitive post[73] compiling all possible pitch sentence types. (I specify that because you never know when someone will top it.) This helps you identify your target audience, which will help you figure out how you should angle your 1. blurb, 2. cover, and 3. metadata.

3. **The cover blurb**: Write this for your story or nonfiction piece. Pitches are short, most often three-ish paragraphs long, and capture the primary conflict of the story or the primary focus and intention of the piece. (This can also be what goes in the query letter.) If you can't come up with this, you 1. are missing a plot or purpose, 2. have a tangled mess of plots and purposes, or 3. (least likely) be unaware of your plot or purpose.

4. **The structural plan**: Take a basic plan of the points involved in three-act structure (or however many "acts" you want to use) and make sure your story fits the structure before you start writing it. If it doesn't, you can 1. change it to fit, 2. pick a different structure to fit it in, or 3. go back to the drawing board.

5. **The rough plan**: Jot down, in order, your goals for the story—what you specifically want the story to accomplish. This may involve the plot, characters, situations, themes, etc. Make sure the goals line up. (For example, if your theme is that

---

[73] http://jamigold.com/2012/01/pitch-prep-how-to-write-a-pitch/

some sins can't be forgiven, making your MC a devout conservative Christian who's theologically required to forgive his enemies may not work—or it might, depending on other details involved. Better to know that up front rather than realizing halfway through that you have to change a devout MC's religion.)

6. **The detailed plan**: Organize your entire story before you write it, breaking it down as far as you want, making sure that each chapter or scene (or however far you've broken it down) naturally leads into the next one. If the flow doesn't work, you can see that up front and fix it, and then writing the book is just flushing it out. (I actually use this for some writing, in the form of a 3x5 card with a sentence per scene, when I know a place or five where my characters will end up but am not yet certain how to get them from where they are to the next place I know they'll be. Though I usually end up deviating from the note cards pretty early on.)

7. **The idea tests**: Jot down all your ideas for scenes, etc., to have in the story, even the contradictory ones. Arrange the ones that fit best for the story you want to tell, fill in the gaps, and put the ditched ones aside in case you need them later. (This one tends to be easiest with note cards, sticky notes, or something comparably straightforward to rearrange and ditch. I tend to do this when I'm doing the previous one.)

8. **The research test**: Research your idea, whether that means conducting researching data pertinent to what you intend to write or researching your competition. Your goals as a writer will determine if a lack or a surplus of results is better. (For example, if 4,747 people have already written books comparable to what you have in mind, you might be pleased at the evidence of a market, or displeased that it's such a well-tapped niche.)

9. **The audience test**: Ask your intended readership (such as your professor, your fans, your beta readers...). This requires you to already have an audience you can ask, but it can work nicely to get an idea—if you're the kind of writer who's more helped than hindered by audience comments on a work in progress. I'm such a writer (which is why I run "First Draft Fridays" over on Wattpad[74]). I seem to be in the minority.

For those timed in-class essays in school, I would jot down bullet points of my possible supporting information for topics, pick the essay topic that I had the best support for, and cross out the non-relevant points. Skip five or more lines to add the introduction later and jump right into the body. Saving the introduction for last is key, I tell you.

That's what worked for me, anyway.

---

[74] http://www.wattpad.com/user/carradee

Have you ever evaluated something you were to write before you sat down and wrote it? What method(s) did you use? What worked for you? Do you have any not-listed methods to share?[75]

---

[75] http://carradee.blogspot.com/2012/02/orient-your-muse-edit-before-you-write.html

STRUCTURAL EDITING: YOUR MUSE'S TRAIL MARKERS

We've already addressed editing before you write, as well as the two different types of editing.

Now let's look into one type of "big picture" editing (also called "macroediting" or "macro editing"): **structural editing**.

Picture your story (or essay, or article, or whatever you're writing) as a nature trail. Some trails are easier to hike than others. Some are more straightforward than others. Some only need you to walk in a straight line, while others require you to hop across a river on some rocks, hoping you don't slip.

Some trails are easy to see, but most will have a specific paint color and pattern marking the trail every so often, on trees or cliffs or whatever is handy at an alert point. (At least, this was my experience in the southeastern US. I'm years out of date, though, because I'm now allergic to the outdoors.)

That trail-marking paint is the *structure* for the trail. The markers must line up and be placed appropriately, for anyone who follows the trail must know where to turn when the trail curves and bends, or when it meets up for a time with another trail. The markers must also match the trail you're on—you don't want the markers defining the novice trail on a trail that involves six days of hiking over rough terrain.

Your story's structure is like those markers. The structure defines the path of your novel—and it often lets the reader know what they're reading (essay, mystery, article, romance, etc.). The structure makes sure that your piece of writing is, in fact, what you intended it to be and not some random blob.

One easy example of the structure as "markers" is in essays, where your thesis must be in the introduction and conclusion (per many definitions of "essay", at any rate), and then the body must have supporting arguments (markers) that are themselves supported by data (sub-markers).

Structure is important in anything, but it tends to be more obvious in nonfiction…to me, at least. In my experience, the structure of a piece of nonfiction will make or break it. You can have the most innovative argument, with the most accurate supporting data, but if you don't structure it properly, you will likely end up proving something other than what you intended.

Another example is the *x*-act structure, used in screenwriting and fiction. (*X* is usually 3 or 4, but there are variants that use other numbers.) Those different points in that structure provide trail markers to ensure that your story actually has a plot.

Plot is conflict. There's a protagonist and an antagonist who are at odds, whose goals each interfere with the other's even if they're not contradictory. The protagonist might be trying to find and save her sister, while the antagonist is trying to seize power by using children like the protag's sister (referring to *The Shifter*[76] by Janice Hardy[77]). Or the antagonist might be a coming flood that's going to wipe out the valley, and the protagonist has to find her aquaphobic daughter and get

---

[76] http://www.amazon.com/gp/product/B002Q1YCYG/
[77] http://blog.janicehardy.com/

her to enter the storm so they can evacuate before the flood comes. (Um, that one's a random example from off the top of my head.)

Plot = conflict = story.

Well, sort of. Fans of vignettes and flash fiction see *story* when there's no plot, but I'm talking about the standard definitions for the majority of English readers. (Some other languages are more accepting of stories that lack plot.) Writers who ignore story conventions might find some folks who love them for it, but they'll still get dissed by readers who are upset for what the story is.

Shoot, even folks who know what they're doing and break the writing "rules" (of thumb) will get readers who sniff and say they have no clue what they're doing. For example, there's an Amazon review[78] for *Hart's Hope*[79] by Orson Scott Card[80] that says "a great storyteller will SHOW me not TELL me what is going on"—as if "telling" itself is an illegitimate style. (If you've not read that book, the tell-heavy style is an integral part of the story.)

Such telling **can** be used properly, by the way. "Show; don't tell" is a rule *of thumb*, not an objective rule.

But this means that the "trail markers" of structure for your particular piece of writing will depend on what, specifically, you're writing. If you're intentionally writing a vignette, you'll have different trail markers than you would for a short story. And a blog post will have different trail markers than a how-to

---

[78] http://www.amazon.com/gp/review/R23RF3RZKBLQU6/ ref=cm_cr_pr_rvw_ttl?ie=UTF8&ASIN=0765306786

[79] http://www.amazon.com/gp/product/0765306786/

[80] http://www.hatrack.com/

article or a research paper. (Thus why I've had to revise the original blog posts a bit for them to even work as a book.)

Different genres also have markers specific to that particular genre. In a romance genre novel, for example, the two lead characters must always be introduced to the reader early on—that's a structural marker that tells the reader "This book is a romance!" They also always have a happy ending (either happily ever after [HEA] or happy for now [HFN]). Mysteries must always have the crime early in the book if not at the actual beginning, and they also tend to feature red herrings. (Red herrings = Rabbit trails that make you think someone else "dun it".)

Can you be innovative and break genre conventions? Of course! But if you break the core rules of a genre, you're writing something other than that genre and will have to be sure your structure (and marketing, and metadata) reflect that.

Genre is and has always been a categorization method to help readers find the type of story they want to read.

So the first step to structural editing is: Make sure your trail markers match your intent for the story—and that they line up in an appropriate order for what you intended to write. If markers are missing, (like "the black moment" in a story or the thesis statement in an essay), then you can add them in. If the markers match something other than what you intended, you then have to decide if you'll market the writing as what it is or revise it to be what you intended it to be.

Make sense?

Can you think of other types or examples of "trail markers" for writing? Have you used this type of evaluation in something you've written?[81]

---

[81] http://carradee.blogspot.com/2012/02/structural-editing-your-muses-trail.html

PLOT EDITING:
YOUR MUSE'S
NATURE TRAIL TYPE(S)

In the previous chapter, we discussed—well, I monologued on—structural editing, comparing it to the paint that marks a nature trail. Another form of "big picture" editing is plot editing, which can be compared to the type of trail you (or your muse) decide to hike.

Plot editing has one goal: to answer *yes* to the question "Does this piece of writing progress logically?"

Does each event naturally lead to the other? Was anything forced? Was anything missing?

In fiction, one way to find missing parts is to look at each event and consider what would happen if that event occurred elsewhere, elsewhen, or to someone else. What *else* could or would or should result?

For example, let's say one character kills someone. What's the logical result in real life? Someone finds the body and reports it to the authorities, and there's an investigation, maybe some arrests and a trial. If that standard due process doesn't happen, why not? Is killing legal in that story "world"? Was it done in a place where nobody would know? Maybe the character *is* one of the authorities, who killed someone in the line of duty (which has its own set of "logical results" that stem from it).

If your story deviates from standard perceptions of reality (insofar as they *are* standard), you need to know it, and your story has to support and explain it.

That means you also need causes and effects, so you also want to look at every event in your story and make sure they fit. You might not reveal everything in order, but everything does have to occur in an order that makes sense.

I could name* one novel, published by the not-so-little publisher St. Martin's (which is part of Macmillan), where the protagonist is (presumably) more aggressive than usual— *before* the event that the book later gives as the cause for her unusually high aggression. Personally, I suspect that error was added in the editing, because the book read as if it had suffered some slashes and rearrangements. But as a reader, I find myself reluctant to try the author again, even though I think it was her debut novel and it had a few more signs of probable editing damage.

Plot editing, paying attention to the *order* of things, is intended to avoid situations like that.

There's a reason that skittish little Evonalé essentially kicks and screams in the end of *A Fistful of Fire*[82]†, but that fit of temper had causes, which appear in the story, and even her temper itself doesn't come out of nowhere.

(I do realize I'm overlapping "plot editing" with "character editing", here. Many aspects of editing are intertwined, where you can fix items in different ways, from different approaches, depending on how you, yourself, work and think.)

---

[82]　http://www.amazon.com/gp/product/B004UMG1PC/

To include that event—Evonalé losing her temper and pitching a fit—I had to previously demonstrate:

1. she had a temper;

2. she would, despite her usual skittishness, blow her top over certain things;

3. the ending event was one of those things that would set her off;

4. she would display her fit of temper that way; and

5. the ending event would actually happen. (Which required quite a bit of setup that I can't describe for spoiler reasons—but several events in the story connect to that one.)

So that fairly straightforward plot event required a minimum of 5 things, depending on how you look at it.

This "plot editing" applies to nonfiction, too.

Cause and effect must line up. Otherwise, your reader's left scratching their head and puzzling over what the heck happened. It's frankly a narrower application of structural editing, and well-structured nonfiction will address cause-and-effect issues in the structural edit. A good nonfiction structure will include proper cause and effect.

Fiction, though, is a harder, because the plot and story structure can be independent of one another. It's completely possible to have a story that fits the *x*-act structure while failing to have the needed logical connections in its plot, or vice versa.

So look at each plot as a trail. Does the trail go back down the same mountain it took you up? Is there a bridge over that stream? Are there gaps in the trail? Does it ever fold back and double up or mysteriously go back over the same bit of terrain?

To be sure, stories can be more complex than nature trails, and they can repeat and double up on themselves like a nature trail can't. Being limited to three-dimensional space, you can't spontaneously walk over the same patch of ground twice without circling around or changing direction.

A story has no such physical limitations. That means it can be a bit tricky, for some books, to figure out when you have a functional trail that connects properly, and when you have redundancies that don't quite work, especially when the timeline jumps around.

But here's the trick: Even redundancies are parts of a linear trail.

Meaning, even though a story trail might have lines or bits that look as though they're going over the same bit of ground again, they can't actually be doing that—it has to be a different point in the trail. It might *resemble* the previous one, or it might even *mirror* something that's come before, but it must still move the story forward.

Depending on your particular story, that might move things just a hair. You might put things out of chronological order, but the cause-and-effect must still connect linearly. *The Time Traveler's Wife* is a case in point, both the original book[83] by Audrey Niffenegger[84] and the movie[85].

If your story has multiple timelines, each storyline is its own trail. But each trail has to intersect or at least be in view of each others' at the right points.

---

[83] http://www.amazon.com/dp/015602943X/
[84] http://audreyniffenegger.com
[85] http://www.amazon.com/dp/B001HN69C2/

How on earth do you do that?

You could plan out each storyline, possibly even more than once, to make sure they fit together properly. You could set up timelines. Personally, I like 3x5 note cards, which you can line up and rearrange so nicely. Scrivener's Outliner function is also easy to rearrange and revise.

But honestly, I personally tend to wing this one until I have some reason to break it down and look more closely. And that's because I haven't found a method that stops my obsessive side.

If I let myself, I'd even make the structural numbers of my story mean something. For example, due to a major event in *Destiny's Kiss*[86] being a seventeenth birthday party, I tried to get it into seventeen chapters.

Fortunately, I'm not obsessively nitpicky, and I can ditch those urges if I can't easily indulge them...but that requires intentional inattention to those things. (That intentional inattention is also why I can be oblivious about dust and mess, actually—because otherwise, I get obsessive about how it *should* be. And then very little gets done because I'm fighting to make it perfect, and I have some health issues right now that mean I sometimes can't even pick up a gallon jug of milk.)

I still want to someday write a story that perfectly parallels word counts and contains a meaningful number of chapters, though.

---

[86] http://www.amazon.com/gp/product/B0058WC3TG/

Do you edit your writing with an eye for cause and effect? Do you have any other techniques to share?[87]

*   I'm not naming the book or author to be polite. I know of other folks who enjoy her, and I did really like one of her related short stories. She writes some memorable characters.

Now, I wouldn't mind another author publicly admitting she didn't care for my books—there's no such thing as a perfect book, and everybody's different; I'm 100% *sure* that some of my favorite authors would hate-hate-hate what I write—but I try to avoid doing things that could be misread or misconstrued or misquoted as burning bridges. If I knew those authors wouldn't mind me naming them, I'd have no problem doing so, just so the curious could check them out and form their own opinions.

†   I am not calling my debut novel perfect. Nor am I saying that it's an ideal example. It's just one that I know intimately, and I've had more than one reader comment positively on how everything draws together and mention that scene specifically as part of that.

---

[87] http://carradee.blogspot.com/2012/02/plot-editing-your-muses-nature-trail.html

CHARACTER EDITING: THE FEATURES OF YOUR NATURE TRAIL

Character editing (which pertains specifically to fiction) could be considered either "big picture" editing or "little picture" editing, depending on what aspect of the character(s) that you happen to be editing.

Either way, the first question that comes into play when character editing is:

DOES THIS CHARACTER WORK, AS WRITTEN?

For my first expanded draft of *A Fistful of Fire*[88], the answer was "No." Evonalé was downright whiny, as one friend told me when she couldn't get through the first section. (If I recall right, she couldn't even get through the first three scenes.)

That whining happened because I had *too* much paranoia in there, too much of one feature. It's like having a nature trail that's in a forest, but 90% of the trees are all oaks. Some folks will still enjoy it just because they like trees, or maybe because they really like oak trees in particular, but people tend to prefer some variety in what they see.

---

[88] http://www.amazon.com/gp/product/B004UMG1PC/

Evonalé's still more self-absorbed and whiny than some people care to read, but it's not nearly as extreme as it was before.

Then there's the question:

DOES THIS LINE WORK, AS WRITTEN?

This question comes in when you're giving the characters individual voices, their own preferred words, their own vocal quirks*—and when you're making sure that the character's coming across the way you intended.

I had to ask that question in every paragraph and line of every scene as I edited *A Fistful of Fire*[89] so Evonalé wouldn't be unbearably whiny. But even that is a little-picture application of a big-picture edit.

Writing *Destiny's Kiss*[90] put me face-to-face with the "little picture" form of "Does this line work?":

WITH WHAT'S ALREADY IN THE SCENE, DOES THIS LINE GO OVERBOARD?

Destiny's Kiss[91] features a vampire, Ambrogino Romazzo, who's...an unusual blend of traits, in part because he jumped from irresponsible *kid* to parental figure for his little sister, who's the narrator's age. The narrator has to figure out if he's a nice guy or a creep, and one little line garnered beta comments that it went too far in the wrong direction.

Granted, I've also received "Ick!" comments on the pair of first cousins who are also a couple in "The Corpse Cat"[92].

[89] http://www.amazon.com/gp/product/B004UMG1PC/
[90] http://www.amazon.com/gp/product/B0058WC3TG/
[91] http://www.amazon.com/gp/product/B0058WC3TG/
[92] http://www.amazon.com/gp/product/B0054GQBLM/

Folks' "too much" meters differ from each other, but too much of anything will wreck your character.

Nice contradiction there, no?

All you can do is make the features balance out as best you can and don't all congregate in a particular section. Vary up the oak trees with maple and apple and shrubbery—and intersperse them appropriately, so the reader doesn't get distracted by a sudden willow where there's no creek nearby to water it.

Having a trusted first reader *of a different background than you* can help find these sorts of problems—because folks with your same background will probably make the same assumptions you do, understand things the same way, so they won't catch when you omit character motivations and such. People of your selfsame background are more likely to understand what you meant, even when it's not actually on the page.

If you fail to include the transitions for folks who don't make the same assumptions you do, can you still find an audience? Sure. But it'll be narrower than it could've been, otherwise.

Have you ever read something where a single aspect or line made the character not work? What about written something where something made the character come across differently than how you wanted? Who caught it?

[93]* As an example of a novel with fantastic individual voices for the characters, I recommend *Chime*[94] by Franny Billingsley[95].

---

[93]　http://carradee.blogspot.com/2012/02/character-editing-features-of-your.html

[94]　http://www.amazon.com/gp/product/B004H0M8M2/

[95]　http://www.frannybillingsley.com/

SETTING EDITING: MAKING SURE YOUR TRAIL EXISTS

This is another item that is more relevant in fiction than nonfiction.

You've probably heard of "setting editing" referred to as *description*. You have to describe enough of the trail of your story for it to:

1. make sense to the reader

2. keep the reader's interest

3. fit your story's point of view (PoV)

It's therefore handy to tackle the setting (the description) as its own round in editing, particularly if you know it's one of your weak points.

What is setting? Setting is your world (where the entire story's set) *and* its locations (where each scene occurs).

So now let's go through these items, one by one:

YOUR SETTING HAS TO MAKE SENSE TO THE READER.

The setting should make sense to you, the writer. It's your responsibility to convey enough of the setting so it makes sense to the reader, too—and in the proper order.

For example, Evonalé in *A Fistful of Fire*[96] can produce purple fire with her magic. Since that's not the usual color that's associated with fire in the real world, I had to make sure that the fire's color was mentioned immediately *the first time she did it*. I couldn't wait until the end of the scene and have it as a punch line. At that point, it would've confused the reader, because the reader would have already built a mental picture of orange fire.

For an example I didn't write, take *The Emperor's Edge*[97]* by Lindsay Buroker[98]. The capital city, where most of the stories take place, is nicknamed "Stumps" because centuries before, a reputably insane emperor ordered all religious statues beheaded…and that's something that's mentioned the first time the MC encounters a headless statue in the story, and *only* then. Otherwise, the detail wouldn't have fit, because the reader would've already built a mental picture of what the statues looked like and any later mention of them being headless would've contradicted the reader's mental picture.

---

[96] http://www.amazon.com/gp/product/B004UMG1PC/
[97] http://www.amazon.com/gp/product/B004H1TDB0/
[98] http://www.lindsayburoker.com/

YOUR SETTING MUST KEEP THE READER'S INTEREST.

That means it has to fit the context, like the aforementioned explanation of "Stumps." It also has to be suitably short and interesting.

In other words, **don't** write an essay or a shopping list—*or* a tirade about the evils of child slavery. (See the next point for an exception.)

Give your readers some credit; they have imaginations, too. A story is also *not* a movie. The reader needs to see the details they won't assume, not every single detail. (For more on that, see Janice Hardy[99]'s post on how much you need to describe your setting[100].)

Exceptions to the previous points come from #3:

YOUR SETTING MUST FIT YOUR STORY'S POV.

Your choice of narrator will color how you must describe things. An omniscient narrator or "distant" PoV can be more difficult to balance, because the narrator's a barely-there objective persona, so you have to carefully balance and consider what the narrator *needs* to say and what the author *wants* to say.

If you write with a "close" PoV—meaning *everything*, even the narrative, is filtered through the PoV character's "head" and "voice"—then you can get away with a lot more. You still must be careful to ensure that things fit and that the description stays interesting, but the character's "voice" help it be interesting.

---

[99] http://blog.janicehardy.com/
[100] http://blog.janicehardy.com/2012/03/literary-tour-guide-how-much-do-you.html

For example, take the character River Tam from *Firefly*[101] (TV series) and *Serenity*[102] (movie). I could describe her as a young woman, a savant, who's been surgically altered by the government to be a telepath and a killer, who lacks mental shielding and whose doctor of a brother gave up everything to rescue her and try to keep her safe. That's fairly short, but it also sounds a bit like a dossier.

If I were to describe River Tam in one of the Destiny Walker stories, Destiny (the narrator) would probably say something along the lines of: "River Tam: neurotic teen with extraordinary reflexes and a knack for killing. Sounds like me."

Destiny wouldn't really be interested in Simon (River's brother) or in the Hands of Blue (the folks who messed River up). So having her mention one of those two wouldn't "fit" the PoV of her novels.†

Do you tackle the editing for your setting? Do you find it easier to establish setting for the "world" itself (big picture) or for each individual scene (little picture)? Do you prefer writing and reading a "distant" (formal) or "close" (informal) PoV?

[103]∗   *The Emperor's Edge*[104] is currently available for free, and I recommend the series for anyone who likes Patricia

---

[101] http://www.amazon.com/gp/product/B004XUMPFQ/

[102] http://www.amazon.com/gp/product/B001HBYHFA/

[103] http://carradee.blogspot.com/2012/03/setting-editing-making-sure-your-trail.html

[104] http://www.amazon.com/gp/product/B004H1TDB0/

Briggs[105]'s traditional fantasy or who is intrigued by the idea of steampunk fantasy.

---

[105] http://www.patriciabriggs.com/

THE THREE TYPES
OF GRAMMAR EDITING

At this point, we've addressed multiple things you should know even before you start trying to edit your own work, along with editing your story structure, plot, characters, and setting. (Specific techniques you'll want to apply when self-editing will come later.)

Now let's leave that "big picture" editing, the macroediting, and turn to the three types of grammar edits: **line editing**, **copyediting**, and **proofreading**. My specialty. ^_^

I say *specialty*, singular, because when you start talking about the type of edits where grammar is involved, definitions and job descriptions overlap. A line editor can resemble a copyeditor, who can resemble a proofreader. (Note that *can*.)

There's also some confusion because many publishers have been cutting staff for a while, so some of them rely on proofreaders to be copyeditors, too, or have acquisitions editors also do line editing. (All those jobs take slightly different skill sets, and the replaced jobs generally get paid more than the ones expected to fill in for them.)

So, either out of concession to the general confusion about the job titles or because they're confused themselves, a fair number of professionals have effactually redefined the terms so now any one of those terms can be used to describe *line editing*.

Here's how I'm describing them:

- **Line Editing** – makes sure your text flows properly and is grammatically correct (for your writing style).

- **Copyediting** – makes sure your text says what you meant it to say and that its grammar and spelling matches the appropriate house style†

- **Proofreading** – is the "Oops" check for grammar (and, traditionally, formatting) to make sure they match the house style†

So as I address line editing, copyediting, and proofreading in the upcoming chapters, please bear my definitions in mind.

> †   A "house style" is the grammar and spelling preferred by a particular publisher, for those items that have more than one possible correct option.

Some grammar rules and some appropriate spellings will differ depending on your grammar handbook and dictionary. Therefore, before you attempt any type of grammar edits, you *must* first decide on a default grammar handbook and dictionary. (I find it helpful to outright read the grammar handbook, too, but that's not everyone's cup of tea.)

Here in the US, the usual defaults are *The Chicago Manual of Style*[106] grammar handbook and the Merriam-Webster[107] dictionary. I use online subscriptions to both. Some types of

---

[106] http://www.chicagomanualofstyle.org/home.html
[107] http://unabridged.merriam-webster.com

writing prefer other references, such as the *AP Stylebook*[108] and the American Heritage[109] dictionary, so what you're writing may affect your defaults.

Oh, and if you have specific grammar rules or spellings for which you'd rather use a different source than your primary one? That's *fine*—

But you will want to make a list of those specific exceptions, called a "style sheet", so you can be consistent. (Other things go on such a style sheet, but I'll get into what those things are, what style sheets are, and some examples on how to make them at another time.)

Most folks are a lot worse at this type of editing than they think they are.

That "a lot worse" includes English teachers. I've had more than one person pitch a fit over my adjustment of their word choice or sentence fragments or some other technique, because there's nothing wrong with that word or technique—*except* they used it overmuch or incorrectly. (Sentence fragments, for example, are frequently *misplaced*, resulting in dangling modifiers[110].)

I suspect the difficulty stems from the detail that it's always easier to see someone else's errors than it is your own, because you know what you *intended* to say and do.

But remember that editing is a skill. Tricking yourself into seeing what's on the page is a skill. Learning to see what you wrote how it actually reads rather than how you intended it to read is yet another skill. All of them are skills with limits,

---

[108] https://www.apstylebook.com
[109] https://ahdictionary.com
[110] http://en.wikipedia.org/wiki/Dangling_modifier

because we're all human and imperfect, but they are skills. *Different ones.*

Don't make the mistake of assuming something's easy for you—Overconfidence Effect in action—and thereby making a fool of yourself.

Do you think yourself good at any of the above forms of editing? Does grammar make you want to run screaming? What's your preferred dictionary?[111]

---

[111] http://carradee.blogspot.com/2012/05/3-types-of-grammar-editing.html

CONTENT & LINE EDITING: "PAVING" YOUR NATURE TRAIL

Trails need some form of paving to exist. That might be a bunch of folks treading over it, to make the dirt stay through the years. That might be asphalt.

But the trail needs *something*, so hikers can, yanno, *see* it.

So. Analogies tend to fail at some point, and here's really where my analogy of your story as a nature trail gets a tad wonky, because I'm having to combine *content editing* (a "big picture" type of edit) with *line editing* (the most in-depth form of "little picture" edits).

Let's start with the definitions:

- **Content Editing** – makes sure your *content* flows properly and is internally correct (for coherence).

- **Line Editing** – makes sure your *text* flows properly and is grammatically correct (for your writing style).

For further definitions, see the previous chapter.

When you look at them that way, my combination of the two of them in this lesson makes a bit more sense, doesn't it? Content editing could be the decision about what type of paving the nature trail will have, while line editing could be considered the verification that the entire trail is paved that selfsame way.

So. Making sure your logistics make sense? Verifying that your character's red hair doesn't suddenly change to blond* for no apparent reason? Analyzing when you need more description, more dialogue, another scene with the two main characters? Noticing that you need more data points supporting your argument or opinion? That's all content editing.

Making sure what's on the page all flows grammatically? That the style works? That your sentence fragments actually are functional, rather than producing choppy writing that's irritating to a reader? Line editing.

Remember my chapter about the two types of editors? Everyone specializes in either "big picture" or "little picture"—and remember above, how content and line editing fall into different "picture size" categories?

That means editors specialize in line editing **or** content editing.

Can a content editor notice and make recommendations that fall under the realm of line editing? Yes.

Can a line editor notice and make recommendations that fall under the realm of content editing? Yes.

But don't confuse the two tasks, and don't expect the same person to be able to do it all. There *is* a difference. Editors (and readers) *do* specialize.

That's why comments saying "This book needs an editor" can be a pain in the neck. Unless the commenter gives examples, you don't know what kind of editing they think is missing—and sometimes, readers pitch fits over things that aren't errors.

Case in point: *Hart's Hope*[112] by Orson Scott Card[113] is *intentionally* written in an archaic "tell"-heavy style, and I've seen a review that called it bad writing *by definition* because of that. Er, no. It's just a non-modern style, which fits the non-modern story.

Fact is, many things called "bad writing" by definition are merely "bad" to *modern sensibilities*, sometimes because they look a lot easier than they are. Newbie writers commonly screw them up. Even so, breaking those "rules" tends to be a bad idea unless you're willing to be publicly ridiculed as an idiot. Even Stephanie Meyer[114]'s overwrought adverb-heavy prose in *Twilight*[115] proved to be good writing for that story, because it connected with her target audience.)

[/end of rabbit trail.]

Of the two types of editing I'm addressing here, you want to perform content editing first. Remember those chapters on editing structure, plot, characters, and setting? Those are forms of content editing.

The line gets a bit more blurry when you're looking at transitions. Transitions between chapters. Transitions between scenes. Transitions *within* scenes. Are they content editing or line editing?

Answer: yes.

Some types of transitions are content editing. (Hey, when did this person enter the hospital? Last I knew, he was in his car.)

---

[112] http://www.amazon.com/gp/product/0765306786/

[113] http://www.hatrack.com/

[114] http://www.stepheniemeyer.com/

[115] http://www.amazon.com/gp/product/0316015849/

Some types of transitions are line editing. (Hey, let's rearrange this sentence so it says that *she* sighed in relief, rather than that the ice-cold table did so.)

That blurred line means that you should consciously look at transitions as part of both content *and* line editing.

Is it any wonder that transitions are often a bane of writers?

^ ^
‾

Line editing tends to work better when it comes *after* content editing. (Why spend time cleaning up a scene that's only going to be redone and re-edited? ...Unless you're like me and have trouble seeing content issues when there are too many typos and line mess-ups.)

Line editing looks at every phrase, every clause, every sentence, every paragraph, every scene—and makes sure the language flows. (And if you don't know the difference† between a *phrase* and a *clause*, you probably have comma splices and other types of run-on sentences in your writing. Just something to be aware of.)

Line editing also considers issues in the writing style. Things can be grammatically correct and still be problematic.

Take the sentence "His eyes dropped to the table." Grammatically, it's fine. Stylistically, it's not.

Why not? It's inherently unclear: Did his gaze land on the table, or did his eyeballs plop out of his head and land on the table? Some readers will get the first meaning, some the second, and some will be confused—particularly when you're writing in a genre wherein the eyeball thing could actually happen. Either way, you're saying the person did not intentionally look at the table, that their gaze focused without their conscious direction. Therefore, such autonomous body parts shouldn't be used in reference to your narrator unless they have limbs like Sally from *A Nightmare Before Christmas*[116] or unless that narrator isn't consciously acting.

Can you choose to write with autonomous body parts? Sure. You'll cut out a portion of potential readers whose automatic comprehension of something tends to be literal rather than figurative, but you *can* do it. Will some folks complain about "bad writing"? Probably. Does that complaint make autonomous body parts bad? No.

Autonomous body parts are "bad" *when they are unclear*.

What's the purpose of writing? To get your point across.

Autonomous body parts can interfere with that purpose. *That's* what's makes them bad writing.

But what if you're using them *intentionally*? For example, what if you *intend* to say that Joe's hand reached for Hannah without him consciously doing so? What if you *intend* to omit the audience of folks who would be confused by autonomous body parts?

Suddenly, there's nothing wrong with them.

A line editor has to keep an eye out for stylistic things like that, which are "soft" (subjective) errors. *And* a line editor has to catch actual "hard" errors, like dangling modifiers. ("Hard" errors are objective, things that are errors regardless of your genre and intended audience.)

Example of a hard error: "Falling hard, the table hurt her wrists."

That sentence says that the table fell hard and hurt "her" wrists. The most likely *intended* meaning is that *she* fell hard and hurt her wrists on the table. But that's not what the sentence is actually saying.

---

[116] http://www.amazon.com/gp/product/B003SI9WYG

That makes dangling modifiers a "hard" error.

What do you think of the blurred line between content and line editing? Which type do you think you're geared towards? Do autonomous body parts bother you?

[117]* "Blond" is the male noun form for the word. If you're using the word as a noun, referring to a female, it's "blonde". In US English, the adjective is "blond", with the adjective getting the "e" added on the end for UK/world English. An alternative in some house styles is to use or omit the "e" based on gender in the adjective as well as the noun. Whichever method you follow, be consistent.

† Short version re: phrases and clauses: A "clause" is a set of words that contains a noun *and* a verb. A "phrase" is a set of words that contains a noun *or* a verb. "He ran home" is a clause, as is "When he ran home" (though those are two different types of clauses). "Running home" is a phrase, because there's only a noun—"home"—and no verb.

Tack an –ing to the end of a verb, and suddenly you have something that can be used as a noun, an adjective, or *part of* a verb. It gets called something different depending on its part of speech. English uses –ing words like some languages use infinitives, which you don't need to worry about unless you decide to learn a foreign language.

---

[117] http://carradee.blogspot.com/2012/05/content-line-editing-paving-your-nature.html

COPYEDITING:
MAKING SURE YOUR TRAIL'S
WHAT IT'S MEANT TO BE

After covering the types of "little picture" editing and delving into what line editing and content editing are, it's time to address copyediting. Some people use "line editing" and "copy editing" synonymously, so let's review how I'm using it:

COPYEDITOR

makes sure your text says what you meant it to say and that its grammar and spelling matches the appropriate house style†

† Defined in an earlier chapter.

How often have you left a blog comment, only to afterwards realize you accidentally said something other than what you meant? Maybe you said Neil Gaiman doesn't write well when you meant to say he *does* write well. Or maybe you post something, only to have the vast majority of commenters make you realize that you effectively said something other than what you intended to say.

Your sentences work. The paragraphs work. The overall post all *works* grammatically—

But they say the wrong thing.

That nature trail you've worked so hard on isn't the path you wanted it to be.

That's where copyediting comes in. Flagging "Hey, did you mean to say this?" and "Where's your source for this number?" and "Hey, why did this character's hair change from black to red?" Sometimes, it's even verifying that the author used the word they intended in a phrase.

Notice that the point with copyediting is **not** "This doesn't make sense," though that can sometimes be a part of it. The point is "Is this what you intended to say?"

For example, to briefly describe the terms, something that's *discreet* is subtle, whereas something that's *discrete* is separate, distinct. The former word is more commonly intended than the latter, so if a writer uses one form of the word, if either word could be used, I'll ask a client which one they intended.

There won't necessarily be anything *wrong* with the sentence, mind you. I'll just be verifying that the client used the word you intended, because a lot of folks don't realize the difference between the two words—and even when writers do know the difference, we still sometimes write the wrong one.

For example, lighting can be either "discreet" or "discrete". Both forms of lighting exist. So if a client says one, I'll double-check that it's what they meant, because that's an easy accident to make.

Editors aren't telepathic.

Hint: That lack of telepathy is why editors might sometimes screw up a writer's meaning. Yes, some editors go overboard. Yes, some editors' failure to understand the writer is not the writer's fault. *But even a good editor might misunderstand a writer and wreck something.*

(And good editors will, yanno, *ask* when they aren't sure— **but** some editors will also ask to *verify* that an author's saying what they intended, so something might not have been wrong with the original writing.)

Editors aren't jealousy incarnate.

Okay, some editors **might** be failed writers and therefore jealous. **Might**.

Some editors **might** try to replace your writing style with their own. **Might**. (Hint: Editors aren't supposed to do that. Ghostwriting practice helps an editor avoid that, in my experience.)

And, to be frank, *every* profession has its share of people who are clueless or jerks. (Tip for writers: do *not* send your copyeditor a rough draft. I once had a few people do that in a row.)

Now. After that delving into the first half of copyediting— making sure your text says what you meant it to say—let's look at the other half. What's "house style"?

HOUSE STYLE

The publisher's preferred grammar, spelling, and formatting.

If you're self-publishing, that means your preferred grammar, spellings, and formatting choices. (Some grammar rules and spellings differ depending on your book—or on your edition of the book. For example, is it "Chris' toy" or "Chris's toy"? Answer differs depending on if you're using *Chicago Manual of Style* 15th edition or 16th edition.)

If you have a publisher, that means *your publisher's* preferred grammar, spellings, and formatting choices. Not yours. Your publisher's.

Why? For **coherency** in what is published.

(Your chapter headers' font size, what you put in scene breaks, that your indents are the same size—those are also part of the "house style", though that's traditionally been more the realm of proofreaders than copyeditors, so I'll delve into that more in the next chapter.)

And, sadly, a lot of companies have laid off their copyeditors, have combined the job with proofreading or line editing, or have so downsized their editing departments that they struggle to keep up with the volume.

Which explains some things we often see in what we read, actually, because some types of errors really aren't visible—or are difficult to see—when you're looking for other types.

How are you at copyediting? Do you know any copyeditors? Have you read anything lately that you think could've used a copyeditor?[118]

---

[118] http://carradee.blogspot.com/2012/05/copyediting-making-sure-your-trails.html

PROOFREADING:
CHECKING YOUR TRAIL
FOR ROOTS
AND OTHER OBSTRUCTIONS

After covering the types of *editing*—line editing, copyediting—we get to the stage that's generally under-appreciated (and often overworked and underpaid, but we'll get to that): **proofreading**.

In our analogy of your story (or other piece of writing) as a nature trail, proofreading is the **final** check, making sure there aren't any roots obstructing the trail, that everything's clean and smooth and what it should be.

Proofreading is the "oops" check.

Proofreading is **not** an edit.

Proofreading is the **final** check for errors.

It's fairly common, these days, for people to combine proofreading and copyediting and require employees to do both jobs at the same time...which actually defeats the point of proofreading.

Some editors even call their copyediting services "proofreading", either out of their own confusion (because their companies told them they were proofreaders due to proofreaders' lower pay), or out of their clients' confusion

(because their clients misunderstand what proofreading and copyediting are, so why bother to educate them on the appropriate jargon?)

Let's back up and define our terms:

LINE EDITING

makes sure your text flows properly and is grammatically correct (for your writing style).

COPYEDITING

makes sure your text says what you meant it to say and that its grammar and spelling matches the house style

PROOFREADING

is the "oops" check for grammar (and, traditionally, formatting) to make sure they match the house style

Look at the name of the step we're talking about: proofreading. That name stems from the publishing world. Before something goes to the printing press, a "page proof" is printed. A "page proof" is a mock-up of what the final book will look like. The "proof reader" is the final reader of the page proof, to double-check for oopsies that have been missed in or added by the editing.

This means that the proofreader often **should** be someone who hasn't been involved on other steps in the process, because the proofreader needs to see *what's actually on the page* rather than what the person *thinks* is there.

By the time you're on the page proof, everything should be done. The only things being caught should be *accidents*, like a typo or a margin issue, not outright problems.

But again, proofreaders are often expected to act as copyeditors, finding and fixing outright problems often for half (or less!) of the pay. Some small presses don't even pay, saying that the proofreaders are getting "paid" by reading a free book.

The assumption is that proofreading doesn't take all that long. In the old-style "oops" check on page proofs, that could be true, because companies often had deadlines and workloads that meant the ones who survived on the job were the fast(er) ones. But...

Proofreading takes longer than reading.

Proofreading takes, *at minimum*, twice as long as reading, not including the time needed to mark up errors. This is even when the work has been properly edited and all that's left are occasional oopsies. (Keep in mind that any found errors have to be marked on the page.)

I'm faster than average. I once worked with several hybrid copyeditor-proofreaders for a company, all of them with more relevant experience than twenty-year-old me had at the time, and they were startled by the quantity I got done. (Folks in Quality Control liked me, too. One introduced me to his wife as "one of the good proofers".)

If a proofreader just has to worry about the personalization, the formatting, and any codes in the documentation—the rest of the piece being canned items—then proofreading is a breeze.

("Canned" means pre-written articles that a company reuses with permission for multiple clients. They're proofread when written, and the proofreader gets used to how they're supposed to look so they only have to glance over things to check "Was anything cut off or improperly hyphenated?")

But if a proofreader has to carefully verify every paragraph for proper formatting, every sentence for proper punctuation, every word for proper spelling—and then notice the surrounding document's formatting, spacing, and font—that takes even longer.

(Have I mentioned my old hobby of identifying font faces and font sizes at a glance? There was a reason for it. I'm out of practice, but as I was writing the original blog post, I was looking at an envelope on my desk that I was pretty sure had some Helvetica in bold allcaps, probably size 14 or 16. It was a piece of commercial mail, giving notice of "Important info inside", and it's obviously sans-serif variable-width fonts. It wasn't Verdana or Impact, and I double-checked Arial and confirmed it couldn't be that font—the *G* was wrong. Per my word processor at the time, Helvetica did look just like what was on the envelope, which might be size 18; I would've had to print a test page to be sure.)

Anyway, this is a *fast* proofreader talking, who thinks it takes twice as long to proofread something as it does to read it, not including the time it takes to mark up errors.

Add in copyediting, and the job takes even longer.

Take a three thousand-word short story. That'll take anywhere from 15 minutes to an hour to proofread, and anywhere from 30 minutes to 3 hours to edit. (Though if it's going to take much longer than an hour to edit, the writer probably needs a tutor, not an editor.)

In my experience, it's actually *faster* to mark up errors on paper. But marking errors in a computer file is more convenient for the integration of those corrections into the final product.

As a result, proofreaders have more responsibility, in a way that makes their job take longer, and don't have that reflected in their pay.

So. Let's back up again.

If a proofreader has to see what's *actually* on the page rather than what they *think* is there, it must be impossible to proofread your own work, right?

Well...

Not necessarily.

It is *possible* to adequately proofread your own work. (Freelance writers often have to do it.) Not everyone is capable of it. And not everyone who *is* capable of it wants to take the time and effort to do so, because it's always more difficult to proofread your own work than it is to proofread someone else's, so it can be more efficient to hire a proofreader and to spend the time you would've been proofreading to write something else.

It is *possible* to trick yourself into seeing the technicalities of what's actually on the page rather than what you think is there.

But then you have to know what it's *supposed* to look like, to know when it's wrong. So the first thing to do is to make sure you know your grammar. *wink*

We'll jump into techniques for tricking yourself in the next chapter.

What do you think of proofreading? Would you prefer to (learn how to?) proofread your own work or prefer to hire someone else to do it?[119]

---

[119] http://carradee.blogspot.com/2012/05/proofreading-checking-your-trail-for.html

METHODS
AND MISCELLANEA

How to See What's Really There (Not What You Think Is There) When Editing the Big Picture

A few times, now, I've mentioned that there are all sorts of "tricks" to being able to see what's actually on the page instead of what you think you put there.

So what are some of those tricks when you're macroediting, editing the "big picture" in your story?

Do something else that'll fill your brain.

Do something mentally intensive, like writing or editing another essay or story, before you go edit the one you've already drafted.

Write (or note card) your outline or synopsis.

Yep, you can write your outline *after* you write the book. Why would you do that, you ask?

- **Reason**: It's easier to analyze a sentence than an entire scene.

- **How to do it**: One sentence per scene. That's the key, see. Write no more than a sentence per scene. Write no less than a sentence per scene. If you cannot write that single sentence per scene, either nothing's happening and the scene needs some revision, or you're getting too wrapped up in the details. (Tip: Drop all adjectives and adverbs unless it's something like "Jane learns Jill is dead," wherein *dead* is an adjective.)

When done with the writing, eye those one-sentence cards with an eye for two things:

1. Does each card describe a change for a character and/or situation?

2. Does each card connect to the card before and the card after it?

No? Why not? Maybe you wrote the wrong sentence, especially if you're just starting out with the technique and getting used to it. Otherwise, that disconnect is a warning sign.

Unfortunately, outlines and note cards[120] are extremely popular at other stages in your writing—like, say, setting all these scenes up in advance. I say "unfortunately" because that means I can't really find the links I'm looking for, though here's one author who uses this method.[121]

In the few months before I first wrote the post this chapter is based on, I know I found a fantastic blog post or three about how to phrase those whittled-down analysis sentences, I think on Janice Hardy's blog...but I changed computers shortly

---

[120] http://hollylisle.com/notecarding-plotting-under-pressure/
[121] http://www.yarnagogo.com/blog/2011/11/how-to-revise-your-novel.html

before writing this chapter and lost my bookmarks, so I can't find it.

Personally, I'm a fan of using note cards in a method fashioned after Holly Lisle's methods: Write each scene on a note card color-coded to indicate how much work is needed. My "color coding" = highlighter or marker along the top edge of a white note card. I also make a key card for that stack.

Reason for the white card, color on top: I can look at the top edge and see how much work the book will need, but I also can read the cards easily—due to a quirk in my learning style, color hinders me. (As an aside, Holly Lisle's book *Mugging the Muse*[122] is well worth getting.)

CHECK YOUR WRITING AGAINST A FORMULA.

Popular ones for fiction include Blake Snyder's *Save the Cat!*[123] and Larry Brooks's *Story Engineering*[124] (Jami Gold offers spreadsheets[125] for those formulas, as well as a few others.)

For nonfiction, the "formula" is more obviously the structure. It'll likely be something like: introduction, point #1 + supporting data, point #2 + supporting data, point #3 + supporting data, conclusion, appendices, references. (Some writers find it easiest to write the content before they write the intro or conclusion. I do.)

---

[122] http://www.amazon.com/gp/product/B007OWGB4G/

[123] http://www.amazon.com/gp/product/B00340ESIS/

[124] http://www.amazon.com/gp/product/B004J35J8W/

[125] http://jamigold.com/for-writers/worksheets-for-writers/

Some authors even develop their own[126] formulas, based on how they see story structure, or based what's popular in the genre(s) they write.

You don't *have* to use a formula—I personally chose not to "normalize" *A Fistful of Fire*[127], because whenever I looked into making it more…conventional, I would've had to make changes that would've hurt what I'd meant it to be.

However, it's highly likely that I unconsciously applied some formula to that story. I have difficulty analyzing plot events and their purpose, but I started checking *A Fistful of Earth*[128] against some of those formulas and found it to be pretty close.

The book-based formulas make it easy: Download or create a spreadsheet for it, plug in your word count, see if the required thing happens at the required page (or ± a few pages), and if they don't match up, determine if you want to change it or not—because formulas exist for a reason, so you need to understand the formula to understand when and if you should break it.

So…yes, I'm well aware that I broke a lot of "rules" with *A Fistful of Fire*[129]'s reactive narrator and meandering story. It also is my most popular title to date, with hundreds of thousands of reads on Wattpad[130], so evidently I pulled it off.

---

[126] http://blog.janicehardy.com/2009/04/sum-of-parts.html

[127] http://www.amazon.com/gp/product/B004UMG1PC/

[128] http://www.amazon.com/gp/product/B009Z54Y8U/

[129] http://www.amazon.com/gp/product/B004UMG1PC/

[130] http://www.wattpad.com/story/4549970

WRITE YOUR, BLURB, TAGLINE, THESIS STATEMENT—WHATEVER APPLIES TO WHAT YOU'RE WRITING.

Key to a thesis statement or tagline is to limit it to one sentence. The tagline can involve some sentence fragments, but you shouldn't have more than one complete sentence in it. A tagline's goal is to cue the reader in about the topic and theme of the story.

Similarly, a good thesis statement doesn't just declare an opinion (like "*Chime*[131] by Franny Billingsley[132] is a fantastic example of how to write character voices"). A good thesis statement includes a reason someone should have that opinion (like "*Chime*[133] by Franny Billingsley[134] is a fantastic example of how to use word choice and sentence structure to produce distinct character voices.")

Your blurb shows up in things like your query letter or cover copy, and your tagline can be a pithy thing you'd want used on your cover or can be your elevator pitch. Writers like Janice Hardy[135] and Jami Gold[136] (and even the former agent Nathan Bransford[137]) have done such thorough jobs writing posts on how to do those things, that I just have to refer you to them:

---

[131] http://www.amazon.com/gp/product/B004H0M8M2/
[132] http://www.frannybillingsley.com/
[133] http://www.amazon.com/gp/product/B004H0M8M2/
[134] http://www.frannybillingsley.com/
[135] http://www.janicehardy.com/
[136] http://jamigold.com/
[137] http://nathanbransford.com/

- Janice Hardy's Query Me This: How to Write a Query[138] (also good for blurbs)

- Janice Hardy's Here's the Pitch—It's a Hit! Crafting Your Novel's Pitch Line[139] (also for taglines)

- Jami Gold's Ultimate Guide to Pitch Writing[140] (also good for blurbs)

- Nathan Bransford's How to Write a Query Letter[141] (also good for blurbs)

Personally, I tend to draft the blurb before I get to far into a book, to help me target what I want my story to be. (For more on how that works, see Janice Hardy's post Query First? The Query as a Plotting Tool[142].)

Do you have any techniques, examples, or resource links that you find particularly useful that you'd like to add? Which technique(s) sound or are most useful to you?[143]

---

[138] http://blog.janicehardy.com/2010/02/query-me-this.html

[139] http://blog.janicehardy.com/2011/10/heres-pitchits-hit-crafting-your-novels.html

[140] http://jamigold.com/2012/06/the-ultimate-guide-to-pitch-writing/

[141] http://blog.nathanbransford.com/2010/08/how-to-write-query-letter.html

[142] http://blog.janicehardy.com/2009/07/query-first.html

[143] http://carradee.blogspot.com/2012/07/how-to-see-whats-really-there-not-what.html

How to See What's Really There (Not What You Think Is There) When Editing the Little Picture

I've addressed tricks for seeing what's actually on the page rather than what's usually there when you're editing the "big picture". Now it's time to cover the tricks to seeing what's actually there—not what you *think* is there—when editing the "little picture".

In other words, how do you see your own typos?

There are several methods, and some work better than others—but the best one for you will depend on you.

Even with these methods, it will take more work for you to see your own typos than it will for someone else to see those typos. You also have to know what you're looking at to even know if a typo is present.

But once you know what you're doing (or if, say, you're writing for school or work and *must* edit yourself), these methods will help you find your own errors as much as you're able.

WAIT BEFORE EDITING YOUR TEXT.

Wait between finishing a manuscript and starting the edit. Ideally, wait long enough that to completely forgot what you intended to write. The length of the original piece of writing, how long you spent writing it, and your own memory will influence how long you'll have to wait for this one to be effective.

This is why a writer might finish a novel and wait a year or more before looking at it again. (Lack of time because they're working on other projects is an unrelated reason writers might wait, but it has the same effect.)

REREAD YOUR TEXT.

The trick to effective rereading is to change the format of what you're writing. If you wrote by hand, read it on a computer or tablet screen (and a sans-serif font like Arial, Helvetica, or Verdana is usually best there). If you wrote it on the computer, read it on paper or your E Ink e-reader (and a serif font like Times New Roman or Georgia is usually best there).

If, due to time or material constraints, you must work entirely on the computer, change the font and change page layout between reads.

READ YOUR TEXT ALOUD.

This means you read it aloud yourself—and yes, mumbling counts. This one is incredibly useful, but it's time-consuming to the point that most people don't find this one worthwhile, except for when they're first playing with sentence flow.

If you read it aloud yourself, tongue-twisters are flags for confusing sentences. You'll also probably be surprised at how much typos jump out at you, when you're trying to say them.

HAVE YOUR TEXT READ TO YOU.

While it's possible that you might find someone willing to read your story for you, this one's usually done by using your computer, tablet, or e-reader. Most systems have a read-aloud function built in, these days.

Even with synthesized voices, once you get used to how ridiculous they can sound when pronouncing things, you can "hear" commas, periods, etc., and find lots of typos. (And if you lose track of what's being said in one sentence…that's probably a confusing sentence that could use revision.)

READ YOUR TEXT BACKWARD, WORD BY WORD OR SENTENCE BY SENTENCE.

This one is commonly recommended by English professors, in my experience. It's designed to be 100% typo check, since you can't evaluate paragraphs this way.

I've only ever done it once for an essay, and I didn't find it worth my time. If you're particularly prone to typos, especially of types that your spell checker won't catch, then you might find the sentence-by-sentence version worthwhile.

USE EDITING SOFTWARE TO FLAG THINGS THAT YOU SHOULD CHECK.

This one can be useful if you know what you're doing, but if you don't know what you're doing, be leery of grammar checkers. They often auto-choose the wrong subject and verb in your sentence, or think that you're using a word as a different part of speech than what it actually is, in the way you're using it.

There are some programs designed with the sole purpose of editing, like AutoCrit[144], EditMinion[145] (my favorite), and Pro Writing Aid[146]. These are best used for flagging for items to double-check, rather than for determining what's necessarily wrong.

If you use Scrivener, you can check the Text Statistics for a window listing how many times you use each word, which is handy for finding words you overuse—or at least that's in the Mac version. I don't know if the Windows version has that function.

USE MACROS TO HELP YOU FLAG ISSUES TO CHECK IN EDITING.

The macros don't do the editing for you—they just check for and flag things that can indicate issues. Jami Gold's post on the topic[147] has the best source post for this, that I've found. Due to certain details in how programs work, it requires Microsoft Word, and it probably works better on Windows than on other operating systems.

There you have it: seven (7) methods for finding your own typos and other "little picture" errors when microediting.

---

[144] http://autocrit.com/

[145] http://editminion.com/

[146] http://www.prowritingaid.com/Free-Editing-Software.aspx

[147] http://jamigold.com/2014/03/ms-word-trick-using-macros-to-edit-and-polish/

What's your preferred method for finding "little picture" errors? Do you have another technique to add here?[148]

---

[148] http://carradee.blogspot.com/2012/07/how-to-see-whats-really-there-not-what_26.html

FIVE METHODS SPECIFICALLY FOR "BIG PICTURE" EDITING

One of the banes of self-editing is that you, the author, know what you *intended* to say, and therefore you have to trick yourself to see what's actually on the page. Every writer's different, so figuring out the best methods for tricking yourself takes practice.)

(And that's in addition to knowing how to edit and being able to edit your *own* writing, not just others'—because it's always far easier to edit others' work than it is to edit your own.)

But how on earth can you trick yourself into seeing what's actually on the page rather than what you *think* is there?

OUTLINE YOUR WRITING ARCS.

For a novel, that's your character arcs, your relationship arcs, your plot arcs, etc. For nonfiction, that might be your themes or arguments and supporting data points.

An "outline" can be anything that charts things out. That might be conventional outline like the one you would hand in to an English teacher, a bullet list, a stack of 3x5 note cards (with one point per card), a mind map (a.k.a. "snowflake"), the keywords in Scrivener… Whatever works best for *you* to see and verify that your arcs fit how they should.

That "what works for you" is key, here. Don't try to force yourself to work with a method that doesn't suit you. That makes much frustration.

Each arc must get a new outline, and it's often best to color-code them. Also, each point *on* the outline needs to indicate where that item is found in the story. (Personally, I like using the keywords in Scrivener to check that characters don't accidentally vanish for most of the book—like Lallie did in an earlier draft of *A Fistful of Fire*[149].)

WAIT BEFORE REREADING.

The wait might be a day, a week, a month, a year—whatever works best for you. (But if freelance writing is your business, you'll want to figure out writing methods that mean you don't have to wait for long. Clients won't give you an extra year on a deadline.)

The wait will help you forget what you intended to write, so you see what's actually there.

This works really well when you write quickly, so the writing gets ditched from your short-term memory, rather than getting etched in your long-term memory. (But this only works if you write fairly clean. It doesn't do you any good if your rough draft is so rough that you can't understand what you intended to say.)

---

[149] http://www.amazon.com/gp/product/B004UMG1PC/

CHECK YOUR WRITING AGAINST A FORMULA (LIKE THE ONE FOUND
IN *SAVE THE CAT!*[150]).

I know I said this before, but plotting naturally follows particular event or emotional arcs. Even nonfiction has chartable flow, if you can eye the text from the appropriate angle. This angle will differ depending on what you want to chart, and it'll come more naturally to some writers than others.

There are exceptions and variations, so figuring out where your particular piece of writing fits—or even what formula to use for it—can take work. And then you have to get the mental distance from your work to be able to identify those major events that fit the formula.

If you go this route, spreadsheets with automatic calculations are your friend for tracking down where those events should be—and if you're an avid reader, you've probably internalized the psychology of plot structure and have hit it more-or-less instinctually.

COLOR CODE EVERYTHING.

Assign colors to different aspects of the writing.

- **Fiction example:** You can put everything relating to characters in blue, dialogue in green, action in purple, description in red… You could then also differentiate between main characters and minor characters, by putting main characters (and their descriptions) in dark blue, and minor characters in light blue.

---

[150] http://www.amazon.com/gp/product/B00340ESIS

- **Nonfiction example:** Thesis and arguments could be purple, supporting data could be blue, and references could be green. You could further break down the supporting data with dark blue paraphrases and light blue direct quotes.

Whether you're color-coding fiction or nonfiction, you don't have to print it out (though you can if you want to). Most word processors (including MS Word and Scrivener) have highlighter functions. Or, instead of highlighting, you can merely change the text color.

If you use this method, be sure to make a key for what each color means, so you don't forget or confuse yourself later.

USE A BETA READER.

When you can use one (and there's no contract or some such thing blocking you), a beta reader can offer a great second set of eyes.

However, you'll want to start by making sure you find the best beta reader for what you need checked. This may mean using more than one—and different projects might need different types of beta readers. (For more on that, you can see my blog post on how to find beta readers[151].)

Bear in mind that you don't want to take advantage of or abuse folks as beta readers. If you try to get folks to volunteer too much of their time or if you're too pushy, you'll drive your beta readers away and not have any for the next time you need them. Show your appreciation for your beta reader by respecting them.

---

[151] http://carradee.blogspot.com/2012/04/how-to-find-beta-readers.html

Also avoid handing a beta reader a story that they'll obviously hate. For example, one of my friends loathes vampires. I used to offer her the chance to beta read some of my vampire stuff, expecting her to refuse, and now I don't even bother. I'll sometimes double-check that she still hates vampires—she does—but I respect her preferences and hand her stories that are to her taste. From what my friends tell me, I'm pretty good about matching titles to their tastes, but it's taken time and practice to get there.

There you go: a brief run-down of five (5) methods to help you edit the "big picture".

Do you have any other methods to share?
What's your favorite—or which do you think
you'd like
to try?[152]

---

[152] http://carradee.blogspot.com/2012/06/5-methods-for-big-picture-editing.html

FIVE METHODS SPECIFICALLY FOR "LITTLE PICTURE" EDITING

As I said in the previous chapter (and at other times), a problem with self-editing is that you as writer know what you *intended* to say, which means you have to trick yourself into forgetting what you meant to write so you can see what's actually on the page.

Writers have different writing techniques and learning styles, too, so one writer's best method might be another's worst. You'll have to practice and test yourself, to figure out the best methods for tricking yourself—and, when you encounter essays or stories that you wrote differently than usual, you'll have to keep practicing and testing to figure out the best route for that piece of writing.

For example, someone who writes a quick rough draft to spew words out on the page won't remember what's there as well as someone who edits while they write. That makes it easier for the former type to trick themselves—but the latter type often knows more about editing.

Because writing and editing are **two *different* skills**.

And fixing what you've written is yet another distinct skill. (Some folks call this revision; some call it rewriting. That's something to keep in mind when people use those words.

Many an online argument would've been avoided if the arguers had bothered to compare definitions, first.)

Also remember: It's always far easier to edit others' work than it is to edit your own.

In the previous chapter of this book, we went over some methods to trick yourself for "big picture" (macro) editing.

How do you trick yourself for "little picture" (micro) editing?

WAIT BEFORE REREADING.

Wait between writing and editing, preferably writing something else in the meantime.

(Yes, this helps both "big picture" and "little picture" editing. Don't worry. This chapter won't completely overlap with the previous one.)

When used properly, this method helps everyone (though it helps folks who write quickly more than it does those who write slowly). Time gives you distance to see what's actually on the page—which makes it helpful for both catching problems *and* for taking a deep breath when you're panicking and convinced your book is the worst thing ever.

(Note: A feeling of "Ah! This is terrible! How can I inflict this on the public!" is *normal*—it's even a **good** sign…)

But you can also cripple yourself with this method, constantly waiting "just a little longer." So it's often best to put a cap on how long you'll intentionally wait before tackling an edit. My personal cap's a month, though I'm an edit-as-I-go type of writer, and sometimes I end up waiting longer just because I'm working on other things in the interim that I want or need to get done before I go back and edit the other item.

(Note: If you're a freelance writer, you'll want to figure out writing methods that let you only need to wait for a short time. Clients generally won't give you an extra year on a deadline.)

It's often best to work on something else while you wait, to help you forget.

CHANGE THE FORMAT.

If it's handwritten, start by typing it; if it's typed, start by changing the font (if not font size or margins) *between every pass*.

Why? It'll move things around, so you have to focus on what you're reading. You won't subconsciously remember the last word on the third page as *on*; instead, it might show up in the middle of the fourth page and therefore reveal itself as an *of*.

Now, when you get down to the final pass, it's best to work on a printed page. A printed page will make it easier to find errors, but it'll take more time to fix those errors. You can print it yourself or set up a POD version on CreateSpace and use that for the final proof.

Barring that, It's best to use an e-reader—preferably E Ink—or a file formatted for publication. However, if you don't do your own file formatting, that can get pricy, because then you'll have to get the file formatted at least twice.

CHECK YOUR WRITING AGAINST LISTS
OF COMMON PROBLEMS.

There are pre-made checklists, like Janice Hardy's "spit shine"[153].

---

[153] http://blog.janicehardy.com/2010/02/re-write-wednesday-spit-shine.html

However, you have "pet" words and techniques and problems, things you're prone to in their writing that aren't necessarily what others have problems with. So as you learn what your weak points are, *take notes*.

Maybe you often confuse *lay* and *lie*. Maybe you like sentence fragments too much. Maybe you find yourself overusing *said* or *–ly* words.

Why do you want those notes? So you can make checklists of your own, catered to your own weak points, to help you make sure you specifically address them.

Then, next time you write something, check it against that personalized checklist.

M*AKE USE OF* F*IND* & R*EPLACE.*

Every word processor these days has a Find & Replace function. Take advantage of it! (Microsoft Word's is the most robust, that I've found. The closest I've found from other programs is in the Mac-only coding application TextWrangler/BBEdit, which can only tackle plain text. I find it incredibly useful for managing my website, though.)

Say there's a word that, while editing, you realize that you're spelling incorrectly or in multiple ways. Make a note of it, then search for it at the end. Also make a note to double-check capitalization and punctuation of things you have trouble with.

For example, some authors have trouble with the capitalization difference in "Say hi to Mom" and "Say hi to my mom." (Notice that there's a modifier—"my"—before "mom" in the version without a capital, and there is no modifier before the version with a capital. It's a quick-and-dirty method of judging if you capitalize the family relationship or not.)

READ YOUR TEXT ALOUD.

This is another one that helps everyone; either you read it aloud (mumbling to yourself) or you let your computer or Kindle or something read it to you. This'll help you *hear* problem areas.

It's also a bit harder to misread that *on* as *of* when a computerized voice says it.

- Hint #1: Anything that's a tongue-twister to say is confusing to read for at least some readers.

- Hint #2: Get out of breath? Your line's too long; it'll lose some readers.

Enjoy those five (5) methods to help you edit on the "little picture" level!

(You might've noticed that I didn't mention using a beta reader for this stage. There's a reason for that. If you don't already know my reason, you aren't an exception to it. ^_^)

What methods do you use? Any here sound like something you'd like to try?[154]

---

[154] http://carradee.blogspot.com/2012/06/5-methods-for-little-picture-editing.html

THE SECRET
OF SUCCESSFUL SELF-EDITING

At long last, after much chattering and discussion and random interruptions, we reach what you *really* want to know: **the** secret of self-editing that *works*.

This secret applies to fiction and nonfiction, to school essays and independent work, when ghostwriting under NDAs and writing under your own name. This secret functions a bit differently in some cases than it does in others, but we'll get to that. (NDA = Non-Disclosure Agreement, by the way; it's a legal document that pretty much means you can't admit you've worked on something.)

Honestly, this "secret of successful self-editing" isn't exactly a *secret*. You probably do this already, without realizing it. I've even mentioned it before.

What's **the** secret to successful self-editing?

BETA READERS.

I hear some of you chuckling or snorting in amusement at how obvious this is, but others are surely startled. How is it self-editing if you have beta readers?

…And, um, if you're not legally *allowed* to have someone else know that you wrote something—as when you work under a NDA—how can you have it beta read? (I'll answer this question later in this chapter.)

First off, when you're at liberty to pick your own beta reader(s), there's something important you must keep in mind, which I mention in the "Warning" section on my blog post on how to find beta readers[155]: **You have to find the beta reader(s) that fit your needs.**

Now, what *are* your needs? That'll depend on you.

Are you weak with grammar? Ask around, try to find someone who both knows what they're doing and who can actually do it.

Maybe you need some translation for a character who speaks a foreign language. Ask folks you know; see if you can find some native speakers to translate the text for you. Do you play online games? Ask guild mates. Hang out on a forum or at a coffee shop? Ask around. You might be surprised by the people you already know.

Me? The rules for commas, for semicolons, for em dashes, for en dashes, for suspension points—I know all that. Sure, I'm naturally blind to my own mistakes, but there are tricks to help with that, which I've already addressed.

One thing I tend to need on early drafts is content comments. I'm particularly helped by easily confused readers, because easily confused readers are fantastic for stumbling over spots where I omitted a transition.

In fact, not all that long ago, I wrote a short story that I knew had problems ("An Invitation Best Tasted"[156]). It was a transition-less mess that assumed the reader was already familiar the world it was set in, and I was pretty sure some of it

---

[155] http://carradee.blogspot.com/2012/04/how-to-find-beta-readers.html
[156] http://www.amazon.com/gp/product/B00I83NXXM/

was out of order. I intentionally found a beta reader unfamiliar with the series or even with me as a writer, someone who would hack my story into puzzle pieces for me.

After that person gave me advice that was completely wrong for what the story was intended to be but that enabled me to see the pieces of the story, I spent well over 2 hours with those original 6.9k words, cutting it into pieces, stitching it back up, and plying it like taffy. I added about 2k new words in that story, but deleted almost as much, so the final story's more like 7.2k words.)

Now, what if I'd handed that mess to a proofreader-type beta reader? That person might've found a few details, and they might've said "I'm confused," but I may or may not have gotten the type of feedback I needed for what I knew needed to be done to fix that story into being what I'd originally intended it to be.

In other words: You must pick an appropriate beta reader for the type of editing you need *for each piece of writing*.

If you don't pick the proper type, you'll be wasting the time and effort of both you and your beta reader.

But even so, contrary to what some folks will tell you, having your story beta read by at least one person who's an copyeditor/proofreader type—particularly if you're already good with grammar, yourself—*can* actually get you a good edit. The problem is that you yourself must be decent at editing, to be able to identify when someone does as good a job as they say they can...and you have to be a pretty good at editing your own work for someone who knows what they're doing to volunteer their time to help you out.

If you're skilled with some form of editing (or a related skill), you can barter with other similarly-skilled writers. For example, when I've needed a content edit, I've bartered and given copyediting in exchange.

You need to know enough about grammar and writing to be decent at editing.

I've encountered many an author who cheerfully had their books "cleaned up" by an editor that they think is *amazing*...until the many typo complaints come in, backed by proof. Or until readers complained about "poor editing" (meaning pacing, or structure, or plotting, or...something other than what the author had edited).

Actually, sometimes authors pitch hissy fits and blame the editors even when the reader complaints address things the editors repaired and the author reverted, but that's another issue.

Regardless of whether you rely on free or paid content editing, line editing, proofreading, etc., you have to know what "good" is for that task, to be able to recognize it when you see it. You will always have to check that your assistants are as skilled as they say the are.

It's as I said in my blog post giving reasons authors should dabble in cover design[157]: Playing with the cover design helps you learn what goes into a cover, and regardless of if you ever get good enough to make decent covers, yourself, dabbling helps you examine covers with an eye for what you want and what you don't want in your covers.

Personally, I prefer covers that have text on top, if not also the bottom. I particularly want the title (not an image) on top, where the eye will be first. For a while, the cover for "Romeo

---

[157] http://carradee.blogspot.com/2011/08/5-reasons-every-indie-author-should.html

& Jillian"[158] violated my preference and didn't "fit" the style of the covers for the related stories, but I also didn't design it. I bought it from Dara England's pre-made covers. (She's currently not accepting new clients, but you can see examples of her work on her site[159].) I've since designed a new cover for the story.

This need for competence—or at least comprehension of what editing involves—is why I wrote this blog post series and now this book. If you don't know what goes into editing, you won't be able to recognize *good* editing of the type you need if you see it.

And believe me, whether you use beta readers or paid editors or both, you need to know what you're dealing with and how to take their input. Otherwise, they might just screw your story up.

But when you pick beta readers (or hirelings) that fit you, fit your story, ones you know how to work with... They can help make your story the best you can get it.

That's why some authors pay their beta readers: gratitude and acknowledgement for the time they spend helping—although some probably also pay because they can't return the favor and beta read for the person beta reading for them.

Now, how do you find a beta reader in situations like school essays or writing with NDA agreements?

In those situations, *you already have a beta reader*: the teacher or client. In some situations, the teacher or client actually starts out acknowledging that the two of you will need a round of discussion to make sure the writing matches expectations on both your ends. In others, the client or teacher

---

[158] http://www.amazon.com/gp/product/B005FA30CA/
[159] http://mycoverart.com/previous-designs/

will expect you to somehow be telepathic and know what they want. (If you get the latter type of client, I suggest you flee a.s.a.p. That stress isn't healthy.)

Either way, it's the teacher's or client's choice for how they want to run their classrooms or business. If you dislike it, try to communicate with them to figure out what they want, or seek another client or teacher.

Just like, in the more conventional sense, you can find another beta reader or hireling when you need one.

Do you rely on beta readers? Do you know what kind of editing you're worst at? Do you know people who can help you with it?[160]

---

[160] http://carradee.blogspot.com/2012/07/secret-of-successful-self-editing.html

WHAT GOES INTO
A HOUSE STYLE SHEET
OR STYLE GUIDE

You've probably heard of making a story or character "bible"[161]: a document (or folder) that contains all your information about your story, from character appearances and ages to backstory details.

(Tip: If you don't have a story "bible", it's a good idea to make one as soon as possible after starting a book. I'm still figuring out the best way to make one for me, so I have a few different types on my computer, just for Aleyi: a "bible" Scrivener project, a Numbers spreadsheet, and a TiddlyWiki[162] file. Each method has its strengths and weaknesses, so I'll probably continue using all three for different aspects of the story.)

But that's a side topic, right now. Most writers know about making story bibles, though I suspect few of us actually make solid ones.

You also need to make a house style sheet (And I don't mean cascading style sheets. House style sheets ≠ CSS.)

---

[161] http://blog.janicehardy.com/2010/03/re-write-wednesday-get-your-facts.html

[162] http://tiddlywiki.com/

A publisher's "house style" ensures consistency across its titles. If you self-publish—or if you want to get your story as clean as it can be for submission—you want to have your own personal "house style" set so your stories can be internally consistent, in grammar and formatting—or at least for consistency within a series.

THE STYLE SHEET (A.K.A. "STYLE GUIDE") ADDRESSES SUCH DETAILS AS...

- Which grammar and spelling styles you use (US? UK? Australian? Canadian?)

- Which grammar handbook do you use? (US default: *The Chicago Manual of Style*[163] [CMS], except in specific fields)

- On what points do you disagree with your handbook, if any? (Create a "writer's punctuation style" list for what disagrees.)

- Which dictionary do you use? (Common US default: Merriam-Webster[164] [M-W], though American Heritage[165] is also popular. Outside the US, Oxford[166] tends to be standard.)

- On what points do you disagree with your dictionary, if any? (Phrasal nouns, verbs, and adjectives in

---

[163] http://www.chicagomanualofstyle.org/home.html
[164] http://unabridged.merriam-webster.com
[165] https://ahdictionary.com
[166] http://www.oxforddictionaries.com

particular differ among sources, and some words even have more than one "correct" spelling in the dictionary [example: T-shirt vs. tee shirt]. Create a "preferred spellings" list for what disagrees.)

• In fiction, who are your characters? (It's best to list your entire cast, with brief explanations when necessary; for example, only one person in *Destiny's Kiss*[167] calls her "Kiss"; others call her "Des" or "Kissy", depending on when they first met her.)

• What special words are in your text, and what do they mean? (For example, in my Aleyi stories, "elfin" is an adjective that specifically refers to people. If I need to refer to something that isn't a person, the adjective needs to be "elven". The word "elvish" should be used only for the language.)

• What foreign words are in your story, what is their language of origin, and what do they mean?

• What naming conventions are to be followed, if any, and for whom or for what regions?

• Is there anything else stylistic or grammatical that should be caught in line editing, copyediting, or proofreading?

---

[167] http://www.amazon.com/gp/product/B0058WC3TG/

Some helpful things to include:

- What do you use to indicate scene breaks? (What character, if any, with how many returns?)

- What's your formatting at the beginning of each chapter? (What font, what font size, and how much white space above it?)

- What's your body text font and font size?

- Do you have any other formatting details in the story, and if so, what are they?

That list of things to include looks monstrous, doesn't it? But formatting this sheet actually isn't all that hard. You can do it one of two main ways:

1. In lists

2. In tables

The main difference is, do you prefer working in a word processor or in a spreadsheet? Personally, I'll use either one. I usually prefer making spreadsheets with Numbers, but in the past few years, the program got rid of some of the features I found most useful. If the style sheet is something I'll be sending to others, I'll write it up as a document in RTF format.

The trick to formatting a style sheet is to use lots of lists and lots of empty space (called "white space" in formatting jargon).

So if you make a style sheet in a word processor, use a lot of bulleted lists, with a bold header indicating what the list is of. Don't try to cram all the information in as little space as possible—that counteracts the purpose of style sheets. Style sheets are meant to be applied, and they're far easier to apply when they're made easy to read.

Here are peeks at of my personal style sheets (for my own stories, so no client confidences broken):

TEXT STYLE SHEET:

Special Jargon and Slang
- **bind-rune** - a magical tattoo that binds the wearer to someone else as property
- **bitch** - (rude) slang for a female shifter; also used by them (not rude) to describe a woman in heat
- **fangface** - (rude) slang for *vampire*

TABLE STYLE SHEET:

Special Words

term	meaning	usage notes
Bridge	in reference to magic: what stage mage someone is (or would be if they used magic); refers to stages where the **person** is in control	
Bridger	someone beyond the elemental Bridge (actively specialized in their magic)	
denfel	elf realm, plant magic	
dentel	elf realm, animal magic	

They're both pretty readable, huh? The spreadsheet version makes it easier to reorganize within individual lists, while it's often easier to rearrange the lists themselves (what order I put them in and how I put them on the page) on the word processing version.

However, though you want things to be simple, you also need to be clear about what your style sheet refers to, so you must begin it properly. Here's the start for my Chronicles of Marsdenfel style sheet:

Notice that the beginning clearly says what world it refers to, what language the story's written in, with the default grammar handbook and dictionary—and notice on that top right. Language morphs over time, so the era of your story can make a difference.

For example, I have plans for stories set centuries before the Chronicles of Marsdenfel. There's one I've worked on a little—because some of those characters in it appear in *A Fistful of Earth*[168]—but I already know that felves were called something else, then, as were faeries. Jargon differed. (It gets a bit awkward when those centuries-old people talk in *A Fistful of Earth*[169], because they actually use some of those out-of-date word choices, so even other characters don't understand some of the things they say.)

You don't *have* to make a style sheet, of course, but I recommend it. It'll make editing and proofreading a lot easier, whether you do it yourself or have someone else do it.

---

[168] http://www.amazon.com/gp/product/B009Z54Y8U/
[169] http://www.amazon.com/gp/product/B009Z54Y8U/

Do you make style sheets for your work? Do you plan to? Do you or will you use a document or spreadsheet?[170]

---

[170] http://carradee.blogspot.com/2012/06/what-goes-into-house-style-sheet-or.html

PATTERNS
IN THE ENGLISH LANGUAGE

English is a "melting pot" language. Though it can be summarized as having a Latinate vocabulary with Germanic grammar, that's an oversimplification.

There's a reason English is often called one of the most difficult languages in the world to learn for a non-native speaker. That's not exactly true, but from what I've studied, other languages tend to have more consistent patterns. I'm not entirely fluent in Spanish, plus I'm out of practice, but I can still hear when a particular verb will be an exception to the conjugation rules, even when I can't remember how to properly conjugate it.

English isn't so simple. Even exceptions have exceptions, as in "*I* before *e*, except after *c* or when sounding like *ay*, as in *neighbor* or *weigh*—and except in certain **weird** words.

There *are*, however, patterns to English grammar. Commas, for instance, often work in pairs. (I intentionally structured the previous two sentences to demonstrate that.) A sentence *always* begins with a capital letter (which produces the rule that any number at the beginning of a sentence must be spelled out, not in Arabic numerals). A sentence *always* has ending punctuation.

There are even patterns to the spelling of word families.

For example, a lot of French-origin nouns have a masculine form and a feminine form, with the feminine denoted by an *e* on the end. I most often encounter *blond* (male)/*blonde* (female), *fiancé* (male)/*fiancée* (female), *chaperon* (male)/*chaperone* (female), and *debutant* (male)/*debutante* (female). But those are hardly the only ones. Others include *brunet* (male)/*brunette* (female), *gamin* (male)/*gamine* (female), René (male)/Reneé (female)…

Granted, the name gender distinction is often ignored, these days.

In US English, the adjective form of such words is usually the male version…and the adjective rules for those words often vary in the various forms of English, but there's a certain consistency to it, within whichever form of English you're using.

So when you're editing or spelling things, look for patterns.

They *do* exist.

Watch for them. It might just help you understand the English language better.

I also find it helpful to think in terms of patterns when I'm picking up words in a foreign language or when I'm creating a fictional language.

Have you ever noticed patterns in the English language? Are there any you find particularly useful?[171]

---

[171] http://carradee.blogspot.com/2012/03/patterns-in-english-language.html

IS SELF-EDITING WORTH DOING? (OR, SHOULD YOU SELF EDIT?)

In all I've said in this book on the realities of self-editing—yes, it's professional to edit yourself[172], and yes, it's *possible* (but not easy) to edit yourself adequately if you follow the secret[173]—I've barely addressed if you *should* self-edit.

Sure, I've said you should *learn* what goes into self-editing, so you can recognize a good editor when you see one, but...

SHOULD YOU SELF-EDIT?

Short answer: Yes.
Long answer: It depends on what you're doing.

For some folks, "self-editing" can end up being a trap, because they get stuck in it *while in progress* on a story (or a nonfiction article or book). There's a reason for the term "*rough* draft", and there's a lot of truth to the saying, "You can't fix what isn't on paper."

Some of us actually have to edit as we go, else we get stuck, so it actually takes us less time to clean up that rough section than it does to try to force rough words on paper, but...

172

173

Folks like me seem to be more the exception than the norm, particularly for newer writers who don't know how to edit yet. And even I've learned how to sit down and force a thousand or three words out, *then* clean them up before moving on. (I do have to clean 'em up before moving on, else I get stuck, but I've learned that because I've tried both ways more than once and timed it. It can be useful to keep track of how long you spend and how much progress you make on things.)

Another factor in self-editing: Why are you writing it?

If you're writing something as an experiment, where you're not even sure the bones are in place… If you can find a willing beta reader who can overlook the grammar to check if the content works, by all means, let them give you feedback before you spend time editing something that doesn't work!

If you're running behind or coming up on a deadline, and your agent or editor or whatever needs to see something— that's another situation where it might be best just to hand them the bare bones before you self-edit, but…that depends on how sensitive they are to grammar errors.

For some folks, grammar errors bury the content to the point that we can't see it well, if at all. Line editors, copyeditors, and proofreaders are particularly susceptible to this, because paying attention to grammar errors is our *job*. We're *trained* to see errors, and turning that training "off" to enjoy a story for the story isn't easy.

Case in point: I'm pretty sure everyone knows what Starbucks is. A few years ago, my family went on a by-car trip out of state, and we stopped at a Starbucks. While there, I picked up a nice-looking nutritional brochure. I examine those, see—those and junk mail and ads and other things, to stay fresh on current trends for formatting and style such things, and to evaluate what works (or doesn't work) and why.

Well, I was eyeing that brochure, admiring the clean lines, the professional formatting, the nicely legible font...

And there was a typo in the first sentence. A comma error, to be precise.

I couldn't verify the numbers and such on all the nutritional information, but as far as the grammar and formatting were concerned, that was the only error I saw in what was otherwise a beautifully done brochure.

I giggled my head off.

See, I have some idea of such brochures cost. After you tally up the artwork, the layout work, the formatting, the writing, the editing, the fact-checking, the proofreading—well, you could probably get a used car for less than what Starbucks likely paid for that brochure. And that's before you add in the printing costs for the good paper (might've been card stock) and the many thousands of copies that were surely made.

And there was a typo in the first sentence.

I expect typos and such errors in materials from small companies, because the *good* writers and editors tend to price themselves outside a small company's budget. When a small company lacks such errors, I'm pleasantly surprised.

But a well-funded company like Starbucks?

I couldn't not see the error. It was a neon flashing sign, a case in point that people aren't perfect.

So you see, even if hire an editor to check the grammar on your work, *you should try to edit it first.*

Why?

So the editor can focus on fixing the errors you don't see.

Think about it. Maybe you know the difference between "break petal" and "brake pedal", but that doesn't mean you'll see it in your own work. (That one was found in *Destiny's Kiss*[174]—before publication, thankfully.)

If your writing is full of grammar errors you could easily fix, that makes it harder for the editor to see the other problems, like the "break petal"s, so you won't get as good an edit—or learn as much—as you would've gotten otherwise. (You'll also probably pay more.)

Note that I'm **not** saying "Work your butt off to get a 'perfect' manuscript before you hire an editor!"*

Frankly, hiring an outside editor is something done by even folks who *can* adequately self-edit, because it's convenient and efficient. Don't underestimate the lure of saved time. Hiring an editor may even be the most effective use of your time and money, too, if you can write enough to earn as much or more than the edit costs you, in the time it would've taken you to edit the work.

If you can't *afford* to pay for editing, or if the convenience isn't worth what you'd have to sacrifice from your budget, don't underestimate the power of bartering or of beta readers, either.

But even if you do all your own content editing, line editing, proofreading…at least get another set of eyes to review your writing, a second opinion, before you post it. Don't post your book for sale and let those readers as your editors. *They paid you* for your book, so as much as you can, give them a book that's enjoyable or functional. (And I say this because I

---

[174] http://www.amazon.com/gp/product/B0058WC3TG/

do know of authors who intentionally use their readers as their typo-finders.)

Readers who pay you are your clients. Show them the respect of offering them the best book you can produce.

Just remember: No book's perfect[175]. So don't make yourself sick stressing over every little comma. Just do the best you can.

And take the things you've learned in writing that previous story (or essay or article or book) and write the next one.

Do you have any more thoughts to add about self-editing? Do you have any other topics you'd like to see me address (about self-editing or other things)?[176]

*   You do want to have a fairly clean manuscript before seeking publication, though, because it's unlikely that your manuscript is so great that they'll look past the unprofessional presentation—and to assume they'll edit a manuscript you submit on spec *is* unprofessional.

("On spec" means you submit the completed manuscript to ask them to buy it; if you've already a contract in place and have a grammar editor lined up, you can be less worried about it, but you still want to give a good impression so they'll want to work with you again.)

---

[175] http://kriswrites.com/2012/06/27/the-business-rusch-perfection/
[176] http://carradee.blogspot.com/2012/08/is-self-editing-worth-doing-or-should.html

AFTERWORD

I hope you've found this book helpful for learning about what self-editing is and ways you can approach it more effectively. Feel free to join in the comments on my blog, and please consider leaving a review to help other readers decide if this e-book is worth the few dollars it costs.

I have nearly a decade's paid experience writing and editing both fiction and nonfiction, and I understand (and can and do often explain) the reasons behind the various aspects of writing, grammar, and spelling. (There are admittedly exceptions, like the fact that, per *The Chicago Manual of Style*, compound adjectives get hyphenated before a noun but not anywhere else, but I still know the rule, even though I dislike it and intentionally ignore it in my own fiction.)

If you like character-oriented fantasy and science fiction, you may also enjoy my self-published fiction. Links to the places you can find me are on the next page.

COME FIND ME!

Twitter: @carradee

Wattpad: @carradee

Blog: http://carradee.blogspot.com

Website: http://mistiwolanski.com/

Newsletter: http://mad.ly/signups/43518/join

APPENDICES

APPENDICES

APPENDIX A:
RECOMMENDED RESOURCES

FREE RESOURCES (BLOGS)

Kristine Kathryn Rusch: http://kriswrites.com/

Every Thursday, Kris posts The Business Rusch, which is always fascinating and educational.

She and her husband (Dean Wesley Smith) have worked in all areas of publishing—author, editor, publisher—for longer than I've been writing. (Which says more about how young I am than about how old they are. I also got a later start than most young writers I'm familiar with, for reasons I won't get into here.)

Dean Wesley Smith: http://www.deanwesleysmith.com/

Dean points out myths and realities in publishing and often even the history behind them.

He's often direct and unapologetic in his views, which rubs some readers the wrong way. He's one of those people who will be intentionally skewed to one side of a spectrum to try to knock some sense into a person's head. (See above note about the credentials of he and his wife, Kristine Kathryn Rusch.)

Janice Hardy's Fiction University:
http://fiction-university.com

Janice has blogged for years, covering everything from practical (and clear!) lessons in grammar to details about specific writing methods. For things she doesn't write or use herself, she recruits guest bloggers.

Trying to figure out what narrative distance is? Need a checklist of overused words? Not quite sure what PoV means? Check out this blog.

Jami Gold's blog: http://jamigold.com/blog/

Jami is unpublished (as of this writing), but she's fantastic at compiling practical information, creating useful spreadsheets, and triggering great discussion (in the blog comments).

Like Janice, Jami also does her best to address all potential methods and points of view, rather than limiting her input to her own pet method.

The Passive Voice: http://www.thepassivevoice.com/

A lawyer's non-legal-advice blog, which compiles references to articles pertinent to authors. He also collects contracts to evaluate, and sometimes posts detailing land mines he's seen, what they really mean, and methods to attempt for defanging them.

This blog is worth following for those contract posts alone, never mind all the other useful things he comments on and links to. And then there are the comments, which can provide an education in themselves.

Courtney Milan: http://www.courtneymilan.com/ramblings/

She blogs rarely, and the formatting can be tough to read, but many of her posts are ones any writer should read, like the one on how to hire a lawyer[177].

Courtney's an attorney or lawyer of some sort, though I can't remember which type.

NOT-FREE RESOURCES

The Freelancer's Survival Guide[178] by Kristine Kathryn Rusch

Single most useful book on freelancing and finances that I've read. An earlier and somewhat out-of-date version can still be read for free on her site.

Holly Lisle's books and e-courses on writing, which cover plotting and world-building and characters and language making and…

You get the gist. You can buy the classes and books from her e-store[179], and her books can also be found on Amazon[180].

---

[177] http://www.courtneymilan.com/ramblings/2012/05/18/how-to-pick-a-lawyer/

[178] http://www.amazon.com/gp/product/0615756298/

[179] http://www.howtothinksideways.com/affiliate/idevaffiliate.php?id=3731

[180] http://www.amazon.com/Holly-Lisle/e/B000APYNNU/

The Copyright Handbook: *What Every Writer Needs to Know*[181] by Stephen Fishman, which instructs on what copyright is, how it works, and what an author needs to understand about it when signing a contract.

Scrivener by Literature and Latte[182], a program available for computers (Windows or Macintosh, with the Macintosh version being the original version and having some functionality that the Windows version doesn't). It's designed for drafting and also happens to be handy for e-book creation. It has a learning curve, but it also has a very generous free trial period where you can try it out, and it costs less than $50 USD.

NOT RECOMMENDED

The Elements of Style[183] by Strunk and White – Beyond the detail that this book only applies to specific types of nonfiction writing, it also claims things that are downright wrong per whatever grammar handbook you want to check. It's worth checking out if you're trying to track down where some of the myths of writing style come from, but when you're trying to learn to write to begin with? Avoid it.

Grammar Girl[184] – I find her explanations often make sense only if you already have some idea what she's talking about. If

---

[181] http://www.amazon.com/gp/product/B005QEQDYC/
[182] http://www.literatureandlatte.com/scrivener.php
[183] http://www.amazon.com/gp/product/020530902X/
[184] http://grammar.quickanddirtytips.com/

you don't understand how grammar works, Janice Hardy's blog[185] gives better explanations.

Appendix B: References

Authors

- Franny Billingsley – http://www.frannybillingsley.com/
- Nathan Bransford – http://nathanbransford.com/
- Patricia Briggs – http://www.patriciabriggs.com/
- Lindsay Buroker – http://www.lindsayburoker.com/
- Orson Scott Card – http://www.hatrack.com/
- Jacqueline Carey – http://www.jacquelinecarey.com
- David Gaughran – http://davidgaughran.wordpress.com/
- Janice Hardy – http://www.janicehardy.com/
- Amanda Hocking – http://www.worldofamandahocking.com
- Holly Lisle – http://hollylisle.com/
- Robin McKinley – http://www.robinmckinley.com/
- Seanan McGuire – http://seananmcguire.com/
- Stephanie Meyer – http://stepheniemeyer.com/
- Audrey Niffenegger – http://audreyniffenegger.com
- Kristine Kathryn Rusch – http://kriswrites.com/
- Sharon Shinn – http://sharonshinn.net/HTML/index_HTML.html
- Dean Wesley Smith – http://www.deanwesleysmith.com/
- Blake Snyder – http://en.wikipedia.org/wiki/Blake_Snyder
- Shanna Swendson – http://shannaswendson.com/

FICTION

- *Chime*[186] by Franny Billingsley
- *The Emperor's Edge*[187] by Lindsay Buroker (also on Wattpad[188])
- *Hart's Hope*[189] by Orson Scott Card
- *The Shifter*[190] by Janice Hardy
- *Sunshine*[191] by Robin McKinley
- *Twilight*[192] by Stephanie Meyer
- The Time Traveller's Wife[193] by Audrey Niffenegger
- Summers at Castle Auburn[194] by Sharon Shinn
- *A Fistful of Fire*[195] by Misti Wolanski, which is also on Wattpad[196]
- *A Fistful of Earth*[197] by Misti Wolanski
- *Destiny's Kiss*[198] by Misti Wolanski
- "Romeo & Jillian"[199] by Misti Wolanski
- "The Corpse Cat"[200] by Misti Wolanski
- "An Invitation Best Tasted"[201] by Misti Wolanski

[186] http://www.amazon.com/gp/product/B004H0M8M2/
[187] http://www.amazon.com/gp/product/B004H1TDB0/
[188] http://www.wattpad.com/story/3815885-the-emperor%27s-edge
[189] http://www.amazon.com/gp/product/0765306786/
[190] http://www.amazon.com/gp/product/B002Q1YCYG/
[191] http://www.amazon.com/gp/product/0515138819/
[192] http://www.amazon.com/gp/product/0316015849/
[193] http://www.amazon.com/Time-Travelers-Wife-Audrey-
    Niffenegger/dp/015602943X/
[194] http://www.amazon.com/gp/product/B000OCXG32/
[195] http://www.amazon.com/gp/product/B004UMG1PC/
[196] http://www.wattpad.com/story/4549970
[197] http://www.amazon.com/gp/product/B009Z54Y8U/
[198] http://www.amazon.com/gp/product/B0058WC3TG/
[199] http://www.amazon.com/gp/product/B005FA30CA/
[200] http://www.amazon.com/gp/product/B0054GQBLM/
[201] http://www.amazon.com/gp/product/B00I83NXXM/

NONFICTION

- *Mugging the Muse*[202] by Holly Lisle
- *Save the Cat!*[203] by Blake Snyder
- *Story Engineering*[204] by Larry Brooks
- The Freelancer's Survival Guide[205] by Kristine Kathryn Rusch
- The Copyright Handbook: What Every Writer Needs to Know[206] by Stephen Fishman
- Janice Hardy's post "Query Me This: How to Write a Query"[207]
- Janice Hardy's post "Here's the Pitch—It's a Hit! Crafting Your Novel's Pitch Line"[208]
- Janice Hardy's post Query First? The Query as a Plotting Tool[209]
- Janice Hardy's post "Tag! You're It: Talking About Dialogue Tags"[210]
- Janice Hardy's post "The Spit Shine: Things to Check Before You Submit"[211]
- Janice Hardy's post "Is Your Prose Purple?"[212]
- Janice Hardy's post "Get Your Facts Straight: Keeping Track of Story Details"[213]
- Jami Gold's post "Ultimate Guide to Pitch Writing"[214]

---

[202] http://www.amazon.com/gp/product/B007OWGB4G/

[203] http://www.amazon.com/gμp/product/B00340ESIS/

[204] http://www.amazon.com/gp/product/B004J35J8W/

[205] http://www.amazon.com/dp/B004A156PY/

[206] http://www.amazon.com/gp/product/B005QEQDYC/

[207] http://blog.janicehardy.com/2010/02/query-me-this.html

[208] http://blog.janicehardy.com/2011/10/heres-pitchits-hit-crafting-your-novels.html

[209] http://blog.janicehardy.com/2009/07/query-first.html

[210] http://blog.janicehardy.com/2009/06/tag-youre-it.html

[211] http://blog.janicehardy.com/2010/02/re-write-wednesday-spit-shine.html

[212] http://blog.janicehardy.com/2010/09/rose-by-any-other-name-is-still-too.html

[213] http://blog.janicehardy.com/2010/03/re-write-wednesday-get-your-facts.html

[214] http://jamigold.com/2012/06/the-ultimate-guide-to-pitch-writing/

- Jami Gold's post "MS Word Trick: Using Macros to Edit and Polish"[215]
- Nathan Bransford's post "How to Write a Query Letter"[216]

MOVIES & TV

- *Firefly*[217] (TV series)
- *Serenity*[218] (movie)
- A Nightmare Before Christmas[219] (movie)
- The Time Traveler's Wife[220] (movie)

MISCELLANEOUS

- National Novel Writing Month – ttp://nanowrimo.org/
- Merriam-Webster Unabridged Dictionary – http://unabridged.merriam-webster.com
- Oxford Dictionaries – http://www.oxforddictionaries.com
- *The Chicago Manual of Style Online* (16th edition) – http://www.chicagomanualofstyle.org/home.html
- *AP Stylebook* – https://www.apstylebook.com
- Wikipedia – http://en.wikipedia.org/wiki/Main_Page
- Dara England, cover designer (closed to new clients) – http://mycoverart.com/previous-designs/
- TiddlyWiki – http://tiddlywiki.com
- The American Heritage Dictionary of the English Language – https://ahdictionary.com

---

[215] http://jamigold.com/2014/03/ms-word-trick-using-macros-to-edit-and-polish/

[216] http://blog.nathanbransford.com/2010/08/how-to-write-query-letter.html

[217] http://www.amazon.com/gp/product/B004XUMPFQ/

[218] http://www.amazon.com/gp/product/B001HBYHFA/

[219] http://www.amazon.com/gp/product/B003SI9WYG/

[220] http://www.amazon.com/dp/B001HN69C2/

www.ingramcontent.com/pod-product-compliance
Lightning Source LLC
Chambersburg PA
CBHW050442290526
45786CB00006B/2132